Praise for Inside the Minds

"What C-Level executives read to keep their edge and make pivotal business decisions. Timeless classics for indispensable knowledge." - Richard Costello, Manager-Corporate Marketing Communication, General Electric (NYSE: GE)

"Want to know what the real leaders are thinking about now? It's in here." - Carl Ledbetter, SVP & CTO, Novell, Inc.

"Priceless wisdom from experts at applying technology in support of business objectives." - Frank Campagnoni, CTO, GE Global Exchange Services

"Unique insights into the way the experts think and the lessons they've learned from experience." - MT Rainey, Co-CEO, Young & Rubicam/Rainey Kelly Campbell Roalfe

"Unlike any other business book." - Bruce Keller, Partner, Debevoise & Plimpton

"The Inside the Minds series is a valuable probe into the thought, perspectives, and techniques of accomplished professionals. By taking a 50,000 foot view, the authors place their endeavors in a context rarely gleaned from text books or treatise." - Chuck Birenbaum, Partner, Thelen Reid & Priest

"A must read for anyone in the industry." - Dr. Chuck Lucier, Chief Growth Officer, Booz-Allen & Hamilton

"A must read for those who manage at the intersection of business and technology." - Frank Roney, General Manager, IBM

"A great way to see across the changing marketing landscape at a time of significant innovation." - David Kenny, Chairman & CEO, Digitas

"An incredible resource of information to help you develop outside-the-box..." - Rich Jernstedt, CEO, Golin/Harris International

"A snapshot of everything you need..." - Charles Koob, Co-Head of Litigation Department, Simpson Thacher & Bartlet

www.Aspatore.com

Aspatore Books is the largest and most exclusive publisher of C-Level executives (CEO, CFO, CTO, CMO, Partner) from the world's most respected companies and law firms. Aspatore annually publishes a select group of G-Level executives from the Global 1,000, top 250 law firms (Partners and Chairs), and other leading companies of all sizes. C-Level Business Intelligence™, as conceptualized and developed by Aspatore Books, provides professionals of all levels with proven business intelligence from industry insiders – direct and unfiltered insight from those who know it best – as opposed to third-party accounts offered by unknown authors and analysts. Aspatore Books is committed to publishing an innovative line of business and legal books, those which lay forth principles and offer insights that when employed, can have a direct financial impact on the reader's business objectives, whatever they may be. In essence, Aspatore publishes critical tools – need-to-read as opposed to nice-to-read books – for all business professionals.

Inside the Minds

The critically acclaimed *Inside the Minds* series provides readers of all levels with proven business intelligence from C-Level executives (CEO, CFO, CTO, CMO, Partner) from the world's most respected companies. Each chapter is comparable to a white paper or essay and is a future-oriented look at where an industry/profession/topic is heading and the most important issues for future success. Each author has been carefully chosen through an exhaustive selection process by the *Inside the Minds* editorial board to write a chapter for this book. *Inside the Minds* was conceived in order to give readers actual insights into the leading minds of business executives worldwide. Because so few books or other publications are actually written by executives in industry, *Inside the Minds* presents an unprecedented look at various industries and professions never before available.

INSIDE THE MINDS

Human Resources Leadership Strategies

Fifteen Ways to Enhance HR Value in Your Company

BOOK IDEA SUBMISSIONS

If you are a GLevel executive or senior lawyer interested in submitting a book idea or manuscript to the Aspatore editorial board, please email jason@aspatore.com. Aspatore is especially looking for highly specific book ideas that would have a direct financial impact on behalf of a reader. Completed books can range from 20 to 2,000 pages – the topic and "need to read" aspect of the material are most important, not the length. Include your book idea, biography, and any additional pertinent information.

Published by Aspatore, Inc.

For corrections, company/title updates, comments or any other inquiries please email info@aspatore.com.

First Printing, 2005
10 9 8 7 6 5 4 3 2 1

ISBN 1-59622-138-0 Library of Congress Control Number: 2005922907

Inside the Minds:
Human Resources
Leadership Strategies

Fifteen Ways to Enhance HR Value in Your Company

CONTENTS

Creating Value through an Aligned People Agenda

David A. Binkley

Senior Vice President, Global Human Resources
Whirlpool Corporation

Creating a Financial Impact

In the last couple years, we've reshaped the role of human resources in our company. The role of the human resources function and mine specifically, is to maximize the performance of the overall enterprise. And we do that by building both individual and organization capability. That's the stated mission of our human resources function.

There are several things we do that have a direct financial impact on the company. The simple answer I could give you would probably be talent, talent, and talent. But that would be overly simplistic. I would say the greatest impact would certainly be in the areas of talent management—recruiting and retaining great talent , diversifying our talent base, making sure that our talent is reflective of the markets we serve at all levels, and fully equipping and engaging our talent.

Under the area of recruiting, we first start off with bringing great talent into our company. We have to make sure we have a proposition that attracts great talent to our company, making sure that our company is appropriately positioned in the market for great leadership talent. We want to be able to, either through external recruiting firms or our own internal recruiting capabilities, know how to reach out and find that talent.

Then, a lot of added value comes from our ability to assess, and be good assessors and judges of talent. I'd say the human resource function, at least in our company, plays a very active role in making sure we have a good story to tell to talent, that we have a proposition in the marketplace, that we know how to find it, and we know how to reach out to it. And I think we do a pretty good job at assessing and bringing talent into the company.

We have a lot of different ways we diversify our talent base. But primarily in the US, we make sure we participate where great diverse talent resides, whether that's at the National Black MBA, or other diversity recruiting forums, or just through the demands we put on our recruiting firms to make sure we're really participating broadly in the marketplace for diverse talent and that the people we see are diverse. I'd say those are the main ways. We reach out; we look for it. There is incredible talent out there that's diverse, that's reflective of our customer base, and we actively reach out to it.

The equipping part is really making sure, if it is leadership talent, that we're building appropriate leadership skills, so our leaders aren't just leaders of tasks, but they're really leaders of people. We have to equip them with appropriate leadership skills so they're engaging the teams and those individuals working for them. If they're sales people, or classical marketing brand people, we have to teach them about our customers, teach them consumer-based skills, so we are really equipping them to carry out the work that they have.

As it relates to engaging them, we have a climate survey that we administer globally called an engagement survey. It's an online survey that's in twelve languages, and we administer that to about 18,000 people worldwide. Then we do a pulse survey once a year to a smaller group, about one-third that size, again worldwide. We've defined the drivers of engagement in our company, and we survey against our progress to make sure the trends are tracking in the right direction and that we take appropriate action against whatever driver it may be. Whether that's an inclusion driver, whether that's professional development, organizational leadership, these are examples of drivers that we identified that determine levels of engagement in our company. It's not terribly different than what you would see at most companies. People want to be included and have the ability to contribute to their fullest potential.

Besides the big impact HR functions can contribute from talent management, we clearly have a role in strategic health care management. In most large corporations, human resource functions like ours manage a great deal of expense, such as active and retiree medical & pension plans. These are huge liabilities on the company's balance sheet. Our ability to be value-added experts in these areas, to control costs and make sure that we have competitive offerings, while at the same time making sure that we're looking at them in a real value-added, resource-creation way, is an incredible opportunity from a financial perspective.

The Art of HR: How to be Successful

The art of human resources is similar to that of a conductor leading an orchestra, where their goal is to get alignment, so all the pieces are playing in a very aligned, kind of harmonious way. When I think of what our best human resources people do in the organization, they make sure that the organization goals are well understood, that people know what their roles are, that we have the right musicians, or talent, if you will, in the roles, and that we're able to put that whole thing together in such a way where we can maximize performance of the whole enterprise. So in many respects, I think the art of human resources is driving alignment, which is not terribly different than what a conductor tries to do with a band or an orchestra.

In order to be successful, I believe an HR executive should have, first and foremost, an extremely high level of trust. The only thing you have at the end of the day is what comes out of your mouth. Your ethics, your standards, and your ability for people to trust and confide in you and believe in what you're saying are what matters most.

They also need very good business skills. They need to understand the priorities of the business, what we're trying to accomplish. They need to have a shareholder's perspective and at the same time an employee champion perspective; you need to always balance those two and understand them both and how they must exist in a very natural way.

Unique Strategies

We're in a very difficult industry, but I don't think there are a lot of easy ones out there. Our industry is very challenging, but I can't think of anything that is necessarily unique from an HR perspective to just our industry. If there were anything, it would probably be what I refer to as HR scrap. Given the competitive nature of our business, we don't have the luxury of making up HR programs of the month or implementing multiple initiatives throughout the organization. A lot of times, these initiatives become scrap after a year or two. So given the sharpness we need to have on value-creation, what we do and what we do for a living needs to be compelling from a value-add standpoint. But I think that's true in most industries.

I would say that the approach I have always taken gets more and more important as our company becomes more global and more complex. I spend a lot of time up-front creating a very business-focused, value-added people agenda. I do that with our senior leaders & human resources team from around the world and with people who are thought or opinion leaders in the company. The key elements of our global people agenda are:

- Developing individual and organizational capacity/capability
- Building employee engagement to work and strategy
- Ensuring all leaders and employees are equipped and successful

I think once you really have a compelling agenda that fits with the business, then you must spend the appropriate amount of time aligning people to it. Then it's amazing to me how good people always line up and want to work on good things.

If you have a value-added agenda that you spend the appropriate time up front working on, I think you need to spend a lot less time on how that specifically translates in whatever country in the world. The up-front energy you spend on really driving a people agenda that brings a great deal of value, and once you align people to it, then I think you can just get out of their way. You don't need to chase them down, monitor them every day, build in all types of complex feedback mechanisms, because good people do good things and like to work on good things that make a difference.

Challenges in HR

I would say there's a lot of ambiguity within the human resources profession. We're dealing in the world of people. Although we've made a lot of things scientific, and I think human resources people, including in our company, have done a nice job creating processes, systems, and metrics that we can evaluate to keep track of how we're progressing in a more precise way. However, at the end of the day, when you're in the business of people, people are unique, that's what you value them for, and it's hard to turn this into hard science. This isn't the field of engineering. So I think there's a lot of complexity that comes from that. We do exist and play in the world of people. That's the beauty of it, the art of it, and what makes it difficult and challenging at times.

Creating a Cohesive Team

I would say I work with our CEO most closely, and from there, I would say the heads of the business around the world. They are members of our company's executive committee; they're the regional Presidents of North America, Europe, Latin America, and Asia. I spend a lot of time with our CFO and a fair amount of time with our board of directors. And, of course, I work with our HR executives all over the world.

It's very important that I understand what the CEO is trying to accomplish across the enterprise, what his priorities are, how he's planning on going about implementing those, what his current thinking is about the business and about the leadership team of the business, things that worry him, thin gs that he's feeling good about. So I need to stay lockstep with him in how he's thinking about the business and where he wants to take it, in order to bring the maximum value from my role.

With everyone I work with, I need to understand their priorities, understand how they're thinking about the business. The CFO partnership becomes a little different, in that, as I mentioned previously, the human resources function is involved in managing huge financial obligations – pensions, retiree medical, health care costs – that the partnership with the CFO, and in our case his people, and determining how to work collectively and together on those big balance sheet items, makes the relationship a little more unique.

When it comes to our HR team, I look for people who really want to make a big impact. What I've noticed over the years is there are a lot of good HR people. The difference between good HR people and great HR people is great HR people really want to spend the time to figure out where they can make the biggest difference. That's very important to them. They have an edge about them; they want to figure out where to play, because you can get pulled into a lot of things as a human resource person, but the real good ones figure out where their real impact comes from.

We have a lot of functional things that we look at, but what separates the good ones from the great ones, in my opinion, is they live, breathe, and create a culture of talent. And it's so clear too. That's what they talk about; that's where they spend their time. They know how to assess talent; they spend their time always building the capability and the competency to attract, retain & develop great talent, and it's so clear and obvious that others know that about them too. They just breathe talent. It's what they're about. They spend their time there.

As I previously discussed, we create a cohesive HR team through the development and execution of our aligned people agenda. We spend our time in the front-end creating a people agenda, linking it to the company's strategy, making sure it's very well connected to the strategic issues of the company, so as an HR team we understand where we bring value, and our goals come directly from there.

Throughout the year, both in face-to-face meetings around the globe, as well as bringing the HR leadership group together, and our monthly teleconferences, we keep track and monitor the progress on how we're doing on leading our agenda.

The Changing Role of HR

I think the whole field is being held to a much higher standard, with ever increasing expectations from the business. That's clear from all the literature, and from external surveys that there's a much more dynamic and important role for both the CEO and the human resource function to play in leading a people agenda. So it's very clear that there is and will continue to be a much higher standard.

I think there will be expectations of the human resources person to be able to deliver greater value, less on the transaction part, because I think you're going to continue to see the trend of more and more outsourcing of transactional-based HR work. But you'll see that the value-added component of HR work is going to continue to grow.

And I think that we'll see that the real true winning proposition amongst companies out there is as they compete and they're able to buy commodities at the same price, and we all have similar business and management processes. We're going to see that it's going to become more and more human capital dependent, which is a very key place for great human resources leaders to play. So I think the standard is just going to continue to go up, for the function, the expectations of the function, and therefore the expectations of human resource leaders. And I hope that's true, by the way.

Golden Rules

- Figure out where you can derive the most value.
- Align your agenda with the business. Figure out what it is, make sure that's aligned with the business and the leadership, because most good HR work gets done through business leadership, as opposed to human resources people all by themselves.
- Hold yourself and others to account for achieving it. Make sure it's very clear what it is, that it's measurable, and that you can hold yourself to account. For example; we hold ourselves accountable to very specific talent management objectives and very specific objectives relating to the financial performance of our health care benefits. We monitor our performance in key areas on a weekly, monthly, quarterly and annual basis just like we manage all other key areas of our business.

A Great Fit

We're in a consumer business. We manufacture, sell and service household appliances. So we're inside of people's homes. People who do well in our company are people who value that, who think it's important. They understand the role we play in our consumer's lives. Whether it's in the area of fabric care, or whether it's our cooking products, whether it's the KitchenAid brand or the Whirlpool brand, they value what our customers do. They're consumers themselves, and they understand the importance and can relate to our customer base. That's very important for us that people value the business the company's in, that they can connect and relate to it, and place a value on it.

Another thing is we put a lot of value on people who like to work with other people. We are a team company. People who like to go it alone probably do not do well here. We place a lot of value on integrity and ethics. We have a saying that there is no right way to do a wrong thing. So people who have a high level of integrity and ethics, who like to work with other people, who value what we do for a living, and understand and can connect and relate to it, those people tend to fit in pretty well in our company. They fit our values.

When we are hiring external talent, we hire people who want to fit with our culture and our values. We make sure they like and respect our business. We make sure that they have the right level of integrity and values, so they fit in, but then we also interview for whatever the functional requirements of the role are, whether it's finance, brand marketing or human resources. We want to make sure that they are bringing the right level of discipline and functional expertise to it.

What to Ask, What to Look For

I don't personally have any favorite questions, although, I do focus in on the leadership dimension. I interview for a variety of jobs, so I'm interviewing very senior people from different places from around the world. If you're going to be the head of our India business, one of the final screens you'll come in for is to meet with me, our CEO, and other key people. So I might be interviewing a CFO or a supply chain person from Asia or a marketing person from Europe.

My focus is on hiring leaders. So my questions are all orientated around:
- their leadership experiences,
- making sure they value leadership,
- teams they have put together in the past,
- where they feel they have had huge successes as a leader,
- their leadership disappointments
- and what they learned from it.

My questions are all very focused around their leadership.

I ask questions that are open-ended, so I don't get yes or no answers. I force the person to share behaviors or actual experiences they've had. It is very clear from the first question all the way to the end whether or not they are actually describing leadership experiences or whether they are describing either managerial experiences or experiences that they have had themselves.

Great leaders tend to talk about what they've done through and with others. So, after doing this for 20 years, I've interviewed a lot of talent and seen great leadership talent. So you have expectations as to the quality of the answers that you're looking for. Of course, we utilize behavioral based questions and answers for these, too. After a while, you don't have to refer back to each answer because you get a good feeling for how the person ranks on that dimension as relative to other great talent. Especially on the leadership dimensions, it's very clear.

Employee-Company Relationship

I think the relationship between the employee and company is evolving, in that you have to be more tailored because there are more unique relationships. I'm not sure if that's different or if HR people and companies just understand better today that there probably is not a one-size-fits-all; there's a lot more customization in terms of flexible working hours, a lot more customization in terms of where people work, how people use technology, benefit offerings, what's attractive to people as it relates to benefits and other forms of compensation. So I don't know if that's different or not, or if companies and HR people are just smarter in recognizing the uniqueness of the population. The population is more diverse, too, so I think that leads you to different places. I believe as the demographics of the world continue to change that you will see an increase in the need to have a value proposition that you can tailor to a much more diverse workforce.

Management Flexibility

We try to be as flexible as we can with our offerings around the globe. There are limits to it, but we try. The way we manage is through a couple of different ways. First of all, we have an engagement survey that I referenced previously and lots of focus groups. So we try to stay current with our employee population on what they're thinking, and we try to do the same with our consumers. We want employee loyalty and engagement, so we try to stay in touch with employees through surveys and focus groups about their needs, wants and aspirations.

We have affinity groups, such as diversity networks or inclusion networks across the company i.e. the

- African-American network,
- The Women's network,
- The Asian network,
- The Hispanic network,
- The Native American Indian network

That allows us to stay in touch at a very grass roots level. These are all voluntary networks. Anyone can participate; you don't have to be of that nationality or ethnic group or gender to participate; they're open to anyone. This allows us, through participation and sponsorship, to get a pretty good and unique perspective into our employee population.

What's Changing?

You are seeing more and more virtual offices, more and more people working from home, more and more people connecting with their work in a very different way. I'm not sure what the next trend is, though, because you saw a lot of trends pop up during the dot-com era, and a lot of those went away. I'm not really sure where this goes in the next round.

I do think, given the changing demographics of the world's workforce, the competitiveness for great talent, and the ability to recruit great talent; it's going to require a lot more custom and unique individual approaches. People have different needs, so that will require a lot more flexibility from employees and employers, and then a lot more unique offerings to really work with people who will bring great value to you.

What Employees Value

We've really spent a lot of time in the last year looking at employee engagement, both inside of our company and externally. What are other companies doing and consulting firms selling in this world of engagement? It's become a little bit of a popular offering out in the market, and the consistent thing I see, with whoever's doing the work, whether it's Gallup or it's Towers-Perrin, very simply, employees want to be included. So I think this whole notion of inclusion, being at the table, being able to participate fully, for me, is the key. You could go on with a lot of other items, but the common one is the ability to be able to make a difference, have a meaningful job that fits in, and be included and able to participate fully in the company.

I don't think it's anything new—I think employees are just able to state it more clearly now. I think employers are able to understand it more now. There were some people, for whatever reason, that just weren't able to participate fully in the company.

I always tell people, "Hey, if you're good, you're going to have a good career here. If you're exceptional, you're going to have an exceptional career here." The sandbox is big—it's a big company; it's a global company. So people can really make a difference here. They can be valued for it. I think that there's this whole culture of teaming, and we don't have a lot of internal competitiveness. We don't compete against each other. In a lot of companies, there's a lot of competitiveness within.

The Progress of Diversity

I think diversity has made substantial progress over the years, but at the same time, I would say it is very hard work and there is still much to do. I think I am speaking generally for society, industry and for us as a company.

Not only can a company specifically strive to be more diverse and more multicultural, but it must. I think it is going to be a requirement for success. The reality is the demographics are changing. If for no other reason, you need to be able to reach out to your customer base. Forget that it is the right thing to do. The demographics and how they have changed in the world would dictate that you need to be more diverse and multicultural as a company. So I think it is non-optional, and the people who are going to win are the people who figure it out faster than the others. Are there things you can do? There certainly are.

It's hard work. I think we are doing many of the right things. In our engagement survey, one of the drivers of engagement is inclusion. You cannot be engaged if you are not included. So we have an inclusion index, and that is within this engagement survey. Again, it is in multiple languages across the company, and we look very specifically at whether or not people feel included. Are they included in their work group? Are they included by their leader? Are they included in the company in terms of decision-making? Do they have a voice at the table?

We look very specifically at inclusion and make sure that people, whether they are in administrative roles, or are of different ethnicity or gender, participate fully in our company. We're able to look across these groups of people and say, "Are there people who participate differently in our company?"

The networks bring value in many ways, they assist in recruiting and they help us with consumer marketing programs. For example, we have a Hispanic network that helps us reach out to an ever increasing Hispanic community in the U.S. They help us fine tune our messages to this important, growing consumer market. The networks help us attract great talent into the company. They actively participate in recruiting efforts across the company. They are out in our communities in a whole array of different activities, whether that is through outreach programs in our communities or education efforts in our local schools.

Our learning on diversity and inclusion is that you really can never communicate enough, because it is a very sensitive topic. It is an issue that society as a whole has, so you are trying to address the societal issues once people walk into your door. They come in the doors in the morning, and all of a sudden you want issues that go on in society to not exist within your company, but people bring their beliefs, their values, and their prejudices, which is who they are into the workplace. Our goal is to educate, have open dialog and discussions around those, and make this a very welcoming and inclusive place for everyone. And we think that not only is it the right thing to do, we think it is a requirement for success going forward, and that the economic benefits are very real.

David Binkley was named senior vice president of Global Human Resources for Whirlpool Corporation in February 2004. In addition, he serves as a member of the company's Executive Committee.Binkley joined Whirlpool in 1984 as regional manager, human resources for the sales organization, and in 1986 he was named manager, employee relations for the Parts Distribution Center in LaPorte, Indiana. Mr. Binkley was named director, executive development, Corporate Human Resources in 1989 and in 1992 he was named director, human resources for Whirlpool Europe (Comerio, Italy). In 1994 he was named director, human resources, Whirlpool Asia (Singapore). In 1995 he was named vice president, human resources, Greater China (Hong Kong) where he had responsibility for Whirlpool Hong Kong, Ltd. and four joint venture operations located in the PRC. In 1996 he returned to Whirlpool headquarters as corporate director, management resources and was named vice president, human resources for North America in October 1998 where he was responsible for human resource activities in the United States, Mexico and Canada. In 2001 he was named corporate vice president, Global Human Resources.

Mr. Binkley graduated from Michigan State University with a bachelor of science degree in business and human resource management, and he attended Michigan State University's Graduate School of Labor and Industrial Relations.

Dedication: *This chapter is dedicated to my late brother, Dean, who mastered the art of engaging people.*

The Woven Path of HR in an Organization

Beth Taylor

Vice President of Human Resources
Thoratec Corporation

The Art of HR

HR is definitely a key business partner for Thoratec and I report directly into the CEO. In my position, I'm ultimately aware of the key strategies of the company and the Board of Directors and the organizational focus required to accomplish those strategies. As our company continues to transform, helping managers navigate through change is very important. We can never communicate enough and must remain ruthless about being close to the pulse of the organization.

There are also specific directives and projects within certain functional areas where I have played a role in helping define direction and outlining a game plan for implementation. For example, we are doing a lot of work around project management and refocusing our R&D organization on product development. I have been an integral part of a team that went out and benchmarked other medical device companies, and drove the process of what to do with all the information once we came back in. These efforts inevitably impact organizational structure.

There are several focus areas within the HR organization that create a financial impact for the company. First is maintaining organizational awareness. This is the pulse of what's going on, which ultimately helps us with hiring, retention, compensation, employee development, etc. We do a fair amount of work in our HR organization with a process we call check-ins. We make sure that we meet with every new employee within the first ninety days to determine how their first experiences have been. We want to know, is the job and the company what you expected? Is there anything you need help with? Are you struggling in your new role? By soliciting this feedback, we are able to identify any issues early on. Additionally, we are able to get solid feedback on the hiring process of matching candidates to positions and outlining realities of the position.

We also meet with a cross-functional representation of the organization throughout the year as part of the check-in process. We target to meet with somewhere around 30 percent of the population. By keeping that process going, we are eventually meeting regularly with most employees.

With this process, I feel I have a read on the pulse of the organization, number one, because I get actual written reports back from that information, and then my HR managers and directors know what's going on as well. Secondly, if we are hearing common themes, we are able to go directly to those functional managers and give them insight, while we are careful not to cross the line around confidentiality and who specifically said what. We inform managers of "common concerns that are being brought forward," which is very helpful to the organization. Quite often these are issues or concerns they are not aware of. This is a way for us to proactively assist in awareness, which helps prevent broader employee relations issues down the road and/or possible resignations. We are also able to get a read on the overall organizational development needs.

The second area where I have direct impact is executive recruiting and building the required leadership to be successful. Being in a growth company, every year we have anywhere from two to three executive level positions become available, either new positions and/or just changes because of the growth in the organization. So it's been an important focus for me.

The third area is a well functioning HR team that continues to run smoothly. The interactions with the HR department ultimately impacts the experience for our customer-base, our employees. It also helps to ensure consistent practices and fairness, which helps prevent potential liability issues that can arise. It also has allowed me to be more proactive in the organization. If I know that I've got the foundation within that core HR function, I'm not having to be off balance and focus too much of my time in that area.

The art of human resources to me means there is no exact answer or approach to what makes you successful or what works for your particular organization. This is similar to art not being created one way and always being viewed differently from person to person.

Successful HR

In my experience, a successful HR executive needs to have a few characteristics. They need strong common sense. A common sense approach has helped to not make business interactions as complicated or difficult. It can be a strong backbone to your decision making process. I've also found strong common sense to be helpful in how you deal with people. It basically helps you think about how someone wants to be treated and what makes them tick. It truly amazes me how many managers struggle with this concept or lose sight of it completely and tend to make things even more difficult than they need to be.

The second competency is financial and general business acumen. I spent the first ten years of my career in credit and collection management and in accounting, and this background has always been very invaluable in helping me understand the full business picture.

Thirdly is strong intuition and judgment. A lot of times the top HR exec is the person in the middle of the organizational teeter totter trying to keep it balanced. It's an invaluable role to provide insight and regular awareness to senior management. Strong intuition and judgment allow you to maintain that delicate balance.

Fourthly, strong leadership capability is important. In order to have the ability to be proactive within the business, you need to have a strong team underneath you that takes care of the daily needs. You should also be the consummate example to the rest of the organization on how to successfully manage a function.

Finally organization skills are necessary for a successful HR executive. Not only are you keeping yourself organized, but you are also keeping major company wide programs and initiatives in place and organized through your department's efforts.

HR Strategies

It's important to build strong business partnerships at all levels, whether or not that's directly being done by the VP or someone within the HR team. Secondly, trust is integral and HR must never lose sight of it. They must continually make sure they are very open minded and honest by approach. Once trust is compromised by anyone in HR it is difficult to maintain organizational effectiveness for the function.

It's important to be able to stay objective. For example, when a manager is putting an employee on a performance improvement plan and questioning the likelihood of the employee's ability to successfully complete the plan, if the manager has little to no confidence in the performance improving, he or she should tell the employee. Be candid and honest. That's a philosophical approach to making sure that people are being treated fairly, but remembering that they are adults and want to be dealt with in a very honest, forthright way.

I found this approach to be counter intuitive for some HR executives because they feel they must cross every T and dot every I and go down a very set path, simply because that's the legal thing to do. Although legal and fair approaches are obviously needed, considering the reality of the employees performance and capabilities, and being candid about their likelihood of not being successful is critical and the most fair approach. I have found most employees in these situations appreciate the honesty and the assistance in working through an amicable transition.

Unique Challenges in HR

We are in the medical device industry and our products are Class III life saving devices. We function as a highly regulated business, so quality and following the rules are of key importance to us. Additionally, the spectrum of the skill set in our organization is very broad. We have entry-level manufacturing roles on up to PhD engineers in our employee base, and that diversity brings its own set of unique challenges. Also being part of a public company creates unique skill set requirements within the role and within how the organization is managed.

From the quality standpoint, we have to be sure that the quality requirements are well understood throughout the organization. We can't have employees making exceptions in this area. This is well understood and very well integrated through the organization at all levels. If someone cuts a corner or doesn't follow a procedure that particular day, it can have dramatic impact, including impact to a patient. So it's important to make sure that's part of the culture and part of the ethics of how we approach things.

I mentioned the diversity side of things; this is not a cookie-cutter organization. If you were dealing with only one type of employee where most of the employee population was in the same type of subset or group, it's a little simpler to approach things. But when we've got the diversity of entry-level manufacturing people who have very basic and specific needs compared to a PhD engineer who's very black and white at how they look at the world, all the way through to all the other folks in between, from an overall HR skill set, it requires solid intuition and creativity. We cannot approach everyone exactly the same because we won't be effective.

Another challenge for HR can often be having a sense or feeling of information overload. You are "in the know" about everything in the business, both good and bad, and you are dealing with employee-related information at all levels. Balancing all this data and what to do with it can be overwhelming at times. Maintaining strong perspective is critical.

And of course, involuntary terminations should always remain challenging. The day it becomes easy and commonplace, there's a problem. You need to always remember you are dealing with a human being and you are impacting their lives dramatically when they are losing their job. I think sometimes you can become numb to terminations when you are in HR, especially if you have to do a lot of it or particularly if you are ever in a situation where you are implementing mass types of layoffs. So I always encourage my group to make sure we are never losing sight of the impact.

HR & C-Level Executive Relationships

I work most closely with the CEO, the Division President, the CFO and the VPs of the organization. It's imperative that I spend enough time with each of these people to truly understand not only their organizational role, but more importantly their current goals and challenges. Quite often people resources and organizational issues are a critical factor in their success. I'm often able to help them navigate many of these issues to prevent some of the roadblocks to success. This can be done through both coaching them directly or through troubleshooting in other parts of the organization.

I describe it as being the backdoor person who is coming in the back hallways, where no one knows where you're going in and out of, but you are maneuvering through making things happen. I think the only way you can do that is by having awareness of the people, what they are working on, where roadblocks may exist and helping managers maneuver through these challenges.

Lastly I believe total cooperation and success truly comes from having complete openness and candor amongst the full management team. So it's trying to make sure there's not a lot of "big elephants" in the room that no one wants to address.

It can be lonely at the top, and the CEO quite often doesn't have a lot of other people he or she can openly talk to. Developing a partnership that allows productive interactions, to openly discuss struggles, being a sounding board and providing information that keeps awareness of what's happening in the organization is important.

Forming a Cohesive HR Team

As I mentioned earlier, I look for HR Managers who are able to function autonomously, and yet have a good sense of when to check in and keep me updated as needed. They need to develop their own judgment on when I need to be involved and when I don't and how to generally keep me aware of what's going on.

Confidentiality is critical. This seems obvious for HR, but I like to function with my team aware of most confidential information. So complete trust and confidentiality is a necessity. I'm very open and my staff knows probably 95 percent of what's going on in the organization. So, I can't be spending time worrying about how someone might handle certain information and they all know and understand the importance.

Customer service orientation is very critical. Again, we have a diverse workforce, and being strong at customer service requires constant awareness of the employees we support and how we approach each individual, which can be very different.

Our organization works by MBOs or management by objectives. So the HR organization has both financial goals, which are the company goals, and we also have very individualized, personal goals that are set at the start of each year. We typically meet two to three times a year to review progress dates, which helps the group stay focused on the higher level strategic initiatives.

Changes in HR

I think the HR role continues to be more and more valued. When a company looks at some of the highest expense lines in an organization, they are people related. Because the people and how they are treated is critical to the success of an organization, the HR function is critical, particularly if they truly do function as business partners.

Interestingly enough, I go back to the basics of what has made me successful and how I manage my group, which includes consistent support and communications. Treating adults as adults and being fair all hold the basic foundation of success in HR. I don't see there being a whole lot of dramatic changes in the direction of HR. I think sometimes we get caught up in the latest and greatest trends, and we start to lose sight of what the core foundation is that makes a lot of HR professionals successful.

I think the importance of HR's role will continue to grow, because more and more CEOs and board members have now experienced working with the strong HR executive and now know the importance and value of their function. They will now begin to expect that strength as part of their team.

Golden Rules

Don't ever lose sight of your common sense and basic intuition. If you are successful in HR, these are traits that you most likely have been blessed with. Secondly, never compromise the trust and respect you build up in the organization over time. Thirdly, figure out a way to stay close to all levels of the organization to really have a tie with the internal realities of the organization. You must figure out what "successful partnerships" mean in your organization.

Training Managers

I think it's important to not take for granted that managers all understand management basics. So, in other words, be sure there is a management-101 type of approach in the training. We went through a fairly big merger back in February of 2001 and basically tripled the size of our employee base, and as we started to finally have an opportunity to put some training in place, we found that you can't assume managers have those basics down.

We happen to have a population too where many managers had grown in their roles over time within very small organizations that had not had a lot of formal training. So we made sure we put those basics in place

Inspiration comes from respect and feeling a following of the managers' leadership and direction. So we focus on instilling this concept into the training.

Lastly, communicate, communicate, communicate, and don't allow speculation. We are very big on having our managers make sure they are keeping people updated.

HR should help provide the tools and come up with the foundation of some type of offering to allow a way for the managers to be trained. It's also critically important that senior management support the initiative and the prioritization of employee development, because you can go out and put all kinds of wonderful programs in place, but if the organization is not ready to dedicate the time to it, it's not going to happen. So it's a combination of leadership by both management and by HR.

Probably the most tangible way that we've been able to measure progress in training is through the check-in process that I described earlier and our employee relations traffic. By staying informed of what type of issues are going on and staying close with the employees regularly, we are able to get further read on the improvement of manager's skills.

Bottom line, it is difficult to place an objective return on investment around training, and we have struggled with having a truly objective way to measure the return.

Training Trends

We have put a lot of effort into both E-learning online, combined with a balance of classroom based training. I'm a firm believer that E-learning works for certain subjects and for certain students, but not for a broad population. So you need to have that approach balanced with classroom based training.

I think the more technical skills, particularly software-based skills, applications that are more tangible and black-and-white, are easier to teach when it comes to utilizing E-learning applications. With some of the softer skills, it's very difficult to take that learning and then apply it. It requires a very disciplined approach by the student to ensure application of the subject matter.

Through the addition of classroom-based training, for example, role-playing or specific assignments during the class begin to allow the opportunity of implementing the learned skill and provide a better blended approach in combination with E-learning.

HR's Role

HR must be in touch with the pulse of the organization. By first building trust within the organization, HR will be able to engage in candid conversation and inquiries throughout the employee base. HR will proactively bring issues and concerns forward and managers will ask for more assistance.

In my coaching with managers, I encourage them to monitor employee's motivation levels based on the flow of work and how smoothly things are being accomplished. How regularly are you dealing with employee-based issues? There are good indicators of that everyday activity, and as long as you are close enough to your employees to know those indicators, you will have a good understanding. So the combination of HR's awareness of issues, along with the manager's awareness provides a strong combination.

HR should be seen as a support mechanism for an employee. This is accomplished by sincere caring, support and follow-through, and through tools and services being provided, not by overstepping areas of expertise. For example, as an employee comes forward with a very difficult personal situation, HR should direct them to some type of help either through an employee assistance program or local services that may be available. HR can also help determine how much the issue may be impacting the employee's work and whether or not it helps to make management aware of the situation.

Often times an employee may struggle on whether or not they should bring an issue forward to their manager or not, and HR can help them think through the pros and cons of doing so or they may even be the person to bring it forward if that's more comfortable for the employee. This needs to all be directed by the employee's comfort level, but HR can help them think through the impact to their work performance or the work environment.

HR needs to be careful not to cross the line where specialized professional help is needed. 'Too personal' is usually defined by how comfortable the employee is in sharing the information. HR needs to be able to meet that need and be able to redirect discussions if they begin to cross the line.

You don't need to know all the details of an employee's personal life, but a manager certainly should have an idea of the basics, enough for the employee to know you are sincerely interested in them as a person and not just as a work resource. Making sure there are regular drop-bys just to say how are you doing or how was your weekend, etc., can bring out a lot of information. Also regularly asking how work projects are progressing and showing interest in their daily work environment is important as well.

My rule of thumb is to try and never let a day go by that you don't at least say hello, or see how someone is doing or go get an update on the progress of a project, which forces interaction on a regular basis.

Ways to Motivate

1. Challenge. One of the firsts ways to motivate, beside through financial compensation, is through the challenge level of an employee's work. Be sure the employee is feeling challenged and learning. This is particularly important for high achievers. Give them exposure to broader projects and

let them contribute outside of their main role if possible. This can often be achieved through cross-functional teams and various special projects that get assigned.

2. Delegation. Make sure you delegate and take a chance, even though the full experience may not be there. Allow your employee to make some mistakes and to have exposure and learn on the job as they go.

3. Employee development. Make sure tools that you are offering employees are there for their personal development. Make sure managers are working with them to stay focused in this area, but be sure the employee knows it's their responsibility to make it a priority. I think a lot of times great initiatives and great programs are put in place, but employee's don't always take advantage of it because it's difficult to continue to focus on development as a personal responsibility to make it a priority.

4. Contribution to the organization. Be sure employee's understand they are part of the pie, that they know how their daily contribution is important. Whether it's between you and the employee or company-wide, make sure you acknowledge when their accomplishments are achieved.

5. Flexibility. Keeping balance in life will keep an employee grounded and then therefore more stable while at work. It's amazing how appreciative people can be by allowing them that flexibility.

Managing with Heart

I believe companies are seeing more and more the value of being flexible, allowing outside balance and the rewards and retention of a person feeling like they are being assisted in balancing all of life's priorities. I think companies are becoming more humanized. However, we also learned we don't have to lose, and shouldn't lose, the basic environment of maintaining core professionalism. A lot can be said for the sense of pride in working for a traditional professional environment.

I think that companies went way too far, particularly in California, where they thought, "we'll just let employees be very free form and not have some of the core basic professional rules of the game." There is a definite sense of pride as that professional foundation has been very effective and proves to be very effective over a long period of time. A lot of companies are putting some of those basics back in place. So I think it's overall a balance between being flexible, being fair, yet not getting so far out there that it's borderline ridiculous.

Companies are realizing that at some point clear guidance on who is running the ship is required and employees are looking for rules and guidance and guidelines and basics. They want to be treated fairly and have a flexible situation, but they are not looking for something that's unreasonable.

I think we could probably debate a little bit about what "leadership with heart" truly means, but based on how I'm interpreting that, I think it has a tremendous amount of potential financial impact from the viewpoint of both hiring and retention. I think that when you are trying to bring people into an organization, obviously a big part of their decision and judgment about whether or not it's a company they want to work for is based on the interactions during the interview, the messages they pick up from everyone they interact with, but also the reputation of the organization and culture overall.

From a retention standpoint, if you can't have a manager who is going to be understanding and provide the balance that I continue to talk about, it's going to be harder and harder to retain employees. When people evaluate the pros and cons of working somewhere, pay is important, but all these other pieces that are more intangible, such as softer areas around "leadership with heart" are critically important to them as well.

Determining Motivations and Incentives

Motivation is a very personal thing that needs to be understood person-by-person or individual-by-individual. Then, quite often, you begin to find commonalities within functional areas. For example, our employees that work in manufacturing appreciate having a clean facility to work in, in a nice geographical location, and there are common desires of just wanting job security, being treated fairly and having the general work environment being good. These are very often employees who may not be as interested in doing other things in the organization and like the comfort zone of the known work environment every day.

So I use that as an example of making sure we understand what motivates that particular type of individual in the diverse business we are working with. Their desires are probably pretty common to peers within the same functional area but it could be very different functional group to functional group. So when you are helping one manager to understand what motivates their team, they've got to make sure they understand each of the individuals, which again typically has some type of commonality to it.

If I consider one of our sales groups, we happen to have highly intelligent, very experienced, highly compensated sales people. It's not a big group; it's about twenty-five people. Their exposure in the industry and their desire to be part of a company that is seen as a world-class leader in the products they provide are characteristics that are critically important to them. So again, it's very different group by group, and I think you have to be very careful about understanding and determining what factors are motivating.

I'm a strong believer in having specific objectives that are monitored and that are truly attainable SMART goals, which is a common acronym. It stands for specific, measurable, attainable realistic and time-bound. This gives you a guideline and an infrastructure to build your objectives around to make sure the objectives meet thiscriteria. I also believe incentives should have some connection to the financial success of the business.

At the lower levels, recognition goes along way. We have a program that our operations director put in place called the Front Runner Program where employees can be nominated by their peers and by managers for awards based on performance. Nominations are based on performance criteria that are particularly important in their functional area such as quality, attendance, etc. So again, that's very specific to the needs of that specific functional department.

Workforce Diversity

How to Define Diversity

You have to be very careful in how you define diversity. Is it simply multi-cultural? Is it a gender mix or is it a background and skill set mix? I think there has definitely been progress in the general sense of the term towards broader diversity, simply by having stronger awareness of the needs. In my experience I don't feel a big gap in this area and/or a need to have an even stronger emphasis placed on diversity in the workplace. I think a company can definitely strive to be more diverse, particularly by utilizing a broader definition of the term.

Being sure an organization is not pigeonholed into too much of a certain "mold" is important. Various backgrounds bring various ways of thinking and creativity, along with helping to define the general work ethic and the corporate culture.

If a company has no workforce diversity, where should they start? Start with the value and the breadth that diverse knowledge and experience can bring to an organization. Come up with an agreed upon definition of what you are trying to accomplish with diversity, and don't just let it be a feel good initiative. There has been a lot of emotional connection with the word "diversity," particularly when referring to ethnicity, and I think a lot of it is making sure a company understands the value of the varying aspects of diversity.

Ms. Taylor joined the Company as Director of Human Resources in November 1999 and was promoted to Vice President of Human Resources in February 2001. Prior to joining Thoratec, Ms. Taylor served as Director of Human Resources for CCI/Triad and was responsible for a division of 1,100 employees. She has also held various other human resource positions such as Corporate Employee Development Manager with Valent U.S.A. Corporation, and as Director of Human Resources with ADP where she was responsible for 1,500 employees.

Dedication: *I dedicate this chapter to my husband Donnie. My partner, my challenger, my inspiration and foundation, my soul mate and true love! Also, to my children, Tyler, Brenna and Paul – you are my miracles!*

The Business of Leadership

Brad Mousseau

Vice President of Human Resources
PC Connection, Inc.

The primary goal of my position is essentially to help the company build a world -class organization that leverages the employee's skills and knowledge. The way I accomplish this goal is by attracting and retaining the right talent for the company, by improving individual capability, by developing effective work groups and by motivating, managing, and measuring performance for the whole organization. I shape the work force to deliver value today and prepare it for the future.

Contributing to Financial Value

Our business model requires talented sales people on the phones calling and prospecting for new accounts. Therefore, the biggest financial impact that I have for the company is getting the right talent in the right place at the right time. This drives our revenue stream. I create an employment brand that interests people in coming to work for us. Having a strong employment brand lowers overall recruiting expense and helps build an employer of choice reputation.

Training is extremely important to financial success. We need to improve employee efficiency and respond to change. Our training organization has a mission to make people productive and affective in their jobs. We measure that success and know the return we get on all our training programs.

The cost of providing benefits continues to be one of the largest cost issues for companies. We continue to control these costs by employee education programs around health care issues and through proper design and management of programs an good vendor relationships.

The Foundation for Success

Human Resources entail the ability to read people well, being decisive, possessing a service mentality and having an eye on the bottom line all the time. A successful HR person needs to be a trusted advisor to all business partners and an individual who is approachable from any level employee. We need to be able to anticipate needs and proactively address them. An HR executive must be a confidant leader with good business acumen skills. Above all, I think we have to be sincere individuals with have high personal integrity and lead by example.

HR Strategies

HR is HR regardless of the industry. A successful person has to learn how the particular business they are in makes and spends money to be successful. I think HR is one of those functions that cuts across industry boundary. I don't think there's any one particular element that's unique to my role in this industry that I didn't have when I worked in other businesses. There may be more emphasis placed on certain aspects depending on the company, but all the basic goals and skills remain constant across the industries. Some companies may place more energy in training/development than recruiting and vice versa, but I don't think there's any one unique thing to this industry.

I attribute much of my professional success to paying attention to the business. I think in any function you have to be a businessperson first and a specialist second; it is critical to understand the business whether you are in HR, marketing or sales.

The way I learn about a business is by conducting a through assessment process for the organization. I look to see whether or not the organization has the right skills in place and then I can determine who we have to hire, who we promote, or who we need to develop and whether we do it internally or externally.

I think the other strategic piece I look at is all based around performance. Are there performance standards for individuals within groups and within the department? How do we get feedback to employees about how well they're doing against their performance? What are the processes that we use to ensure meaningful and accurate appraisals? As a part of this piece, I consider rewards. How do we compensate people? How do we bonus people? Those are the financial aspects of rewards, but there are non-financial aspects as well such as how the company creates meaningful work, recognizes people and celebrates achievements.

Next I examine the organization itself. How is it organized? What is the shape of the organization? How many levels should we have? Who reports to whom? What are the policies that guide the company? How do we communicate with all our employees about policies and how do we build a shared mind set?

The last strategic element I look at is change. How we prepare the organization for change and how will we lead our people through it? How do we drive change in the organization? I consider the effectiveness of leaning or sharing ideas and putting in different work processes.

I have been in HR for twenty-eight years, and I think that early on the function wasn't as respected as it should be. I have always tried to bring a business aspect to everything I do in Human Resources and I think it is important that the role of HR be respected and viewed as a strategic partner. I have been fortunate to work for companies that understand the value of that relationship. I report directly to the Chairman of the Board and CEO and work closely developing organizational strategy around people and new business initiatives. I partner with the CFO to look at incentive programs, pay backs and how we can improve the bottom line. I work with all executives. I work with the subsidiaries almost every day on employee relations issues, compensation issues, structure issues and recruiting issues. I also function as a safe sounding board for other executives to bounce their ideas around in a non-bias environment before they implement.

I think it is important for an HR executive to understand the roles of other people with whom we work. We need to know the business aspect of what they do. They're under pressure to make the dollars, make the sales, and make the net margins, so we have to understand what levers to pull that help them achieve their goals.

The HR Team

Personal integrity is a critical quality of any member of the HR team. I look for people who are self-motivated, have good business acumen and a sense of urgency. HR people need to understand what they do and how that impacts the business.

I also try to find people who think differently than I do because I want to have team members who can challenge my ideas and feel comfortable doing so. That way, what we come up with when we're faced with an issue is the best possible solution for the company. I don't want someone to just sit there and say yes because I'm saying it. I want to have the collegial debate and to go back and forth with ideas and thoughts so that before launch any new programs or initiatives they are well thought out and have a greater chance of succeeding.

Setting Goals

After we understand what the overall company's objectives are for the year, we set our HR agenda to support those overall goals. I have a process that we go through in order to set our goals and we set action plan to achieve them. We set up and agree upon a measurement system for goals and review them quarterly. The annual bonus opportunity is tied to achievement of goals that have an impact on the company.

Sometimes business initiatives change and we may not get everything accomplished that we set out to do for that quarter. I understand that and we make changes throughout the quarter when appropriate. We move goals around and add new ones depending upon how our business priorities change.

The Changing Role of HR

In the last ten years at least, the HR role has changed dramatically. It is now more involved with the overall running of the business. In the future, I think the HR role is going to become even more important. Eventually, companies are going to be compelled to put HR leaders on their boards. The complexities around compensation for executives, stock programs, business ethics, and skilled labor shortages will warrant an expert. That expertise resides in the human resource function.

I think there'll be probably more out-sourcing of the less-strategic jobs so HR will become more of a contracts manager in some aspects. HR will continue to become more valued as a strategic partner setting strategy and developing leaders.

Rules to Follow

The first rule of HR is to deliver value. Understand how you impact the bottom line. For example, from a recruiting standpoint, I like to have a sense of urgency in my recruiters so they understand that when hiring a salesperson, if they can get that person here and trained, then that person can begin making sales and adding to the bottom line. The sooner that person can get on-board the sooner value can be created for the company.

Have a high level of personal integrity and be sincere in everything you do. Never compromise your values.

Be a good listener and know how to probe for the root causes of issues before you act. The first thing you hear usually isn't the full story.

Potential Nightmares

Major Concerns

There are several worst-case scenarios that plague HR executives. One is if we can't find enough talent. As the pool of talented people continues to shrink as baby boomers retire or people make career changes how do you keep your talent pool filled? We need to develop earlier deeper relationships with schools to develop a better pipeline of potential employees. We need to look at ways to changes functions and automate processes so that fewer people are required.

I also worry about leadership development and succession planning. Companies that grow have strong leaders and are constantly developing a leadership pool. In order to continuing growing we need our "unfair share of the talent that is in the marketplace."

Budgeting

I really don't have a lot of budget surprises. I think that another skill that you need in business is anticipation skills. By that I mean that you should not only think about what you're doing now, but think three or four steps down the road. I consider possible problems or issues that may arise so I can create a contingency budget plan. When I do go through budgets, I understand what I can deliver with the budget that I have. Then I design an upside budget in which if X happens, than I need X more resources to make it happen.

We allocate a specific amount for each new hire, salary and training initiative. Most of our training emphasis in the past has been on salespeople, and when we hire a new salesperson we put them through six weeks of training. They are measured, tested and given bonus opportunities while they're in training. There are certain gates that they have to hit such as setting up a certain number of new accounts and understanding how to navigate through our systems. We know each person coming in, how much we end up spending, how long they're in training, how long they go through each step before they hit the sales floor, and then we measure them beyond that so that we understand their productive levels compared to our training expense.

We are in the process of pushing a new enterprise-wide training model through the organization. This program will allow us to measure each individual for leadership competencies and determine what training they need. We know how much we need to budget per individual for training and have developed an ROI measurement so we know how effective the training has been.

Terminations and New Hires

We basically have a three-step process for letting people go. With this model, our whole initiative is not on how to terminate the person, but rather how to make that person successful. Step one is we do a coaching and counseling session with an individual. We determine what roadblocks are preventing them from being successful and can help them overcome the issue. If there is no improvement after the coaching we dig a little deeper and try to understand the root cause of the problem. Is it a lack of basic skills? Do they want to be here? I think the core of our system is that we treat all employees regardless of their level with dignity and respect so that they will leave the organization without feeling embarrassed.

The time it takes to fill a position varies. I think the higher-level positions are becoming more difficult to fill. The officer positions are tough because of all of the responsibility that goes with Sarbanes-Oxley. With salespeople or any others who have a revenue impact on the company, we try to get them in place sooner rather than later. I try to say that we can fill any position within thirty to sixty days.

If it takes longer than planned to fill a position, we try to step up the resources and do an assessment of what we may be missing. Is our advertising off the mark? Is the job something that we just don't have a good skill-match for in this area? Do we need to get outside help to source for this position? Our best source of filling jobs is through employee referrals. If we can create the right environment, we will have more employees referred to us. That's the best method of recruiting that you can have and we today run about 35 percent of our hires are filled through employee referrals. We offer a bounty program for referrals as well.

The biggest challenge in finding the right candidates is getting people with the right skill sets who are motivated to be successful. We want people who are driven, want a challenge and want to grow in their career. We are basically a telemarketing organization, so I have five hundred salespeople and need to find people who fit into the culture of the company. I hire college grads that are successful. I hire people that have been bartenders that are successful. I hire career changers. It's all in how they're motivated. The key to making good hires is making the right assessment up front.

When we need to fill a C-level position, the cultural fit is again very important. In my experience, people generally don't fail in a job at that level because they don't have the skill set. It's usually they don't fit into the culture of the company. You need to spend a lot of time up front testing the culture fit. In addition, Sarbanes-Oxley further complicates C-level hiring. I think C level people will do more due diligence on the companies they are interested in then they have ever done before. They have a lot more at personal risk today then they ever had before and want to know they are joining ethical companies.

The Future of HR

Human Resources is going to gradually become more important for implementing the right measurement systems to help a company grow. It will shift from an administrative role to one that is more of a business-partnership and business-leader role.

The internet has effected Human Resources from a recruiting standpoint in that it has certainly made a lot more resumes available. From a business/company standpoint, we try to drive a lot of our business over the internet, which creates a whole other series of issues at which we will have to look in the future. The internet will allow us to create virtual workforce that will have access to data and processes anywhere , anyplace, at any time. Imagine a multibillion dollar company linked around the world selling and servicing customers 24-7, all tied together by the internet. Companies will still have to keep a human touch by occasional face to face meetings but for the most part it's a way to lower operating costs and eliminate brick and motor expenses. These savings can be used for profit sharing plans, development programs, and new investments.

Working with Other Departments

Giving good advice and counsel is the best way to foster good relationships with other departments. To do that, we need to understand the various departments that we support. We assign HR generalists, or managers, to support each department. They understand how that group spends and makes money and what keeps them up at night, so they understand how to counsel them to relieve those pressure points. It might be getting that next person hired or it might be coaching that bad manager, but they're a business partner to the head of that department.

Employee Loyalty

The Keys to Employee Loyalty

Developing loyalty boils down to a couple elements. The first is having a company with a definite direction and a clearly articulated plan that people can follow. This means having an effective management team that walks the talk, does what it says it's going to do and delivers results. That way, people can believe in them, and that fosters employee loyalty. Providing jobs that excite and challenge employees while offering growth opportunities will also encourage loyalty. Paying attention to how you coach people for better performance and how you reward them is critical as well. The ability to allow people to balance work and personal issues also builds a loyalty that pays back ten fold.

If a company feels it is lacking loyalty, it needs to communicate, communicate, communicate. Develop focus groups to find out what your employees are thinking. Develop programs to address the gaps you discover, and measure your success over time.

The company should do an organizational assessment. They should look at the skill sets, how they reward people, how they built the capacity for change and how they develop employees. Put plans together to start changing your environment. The old saying is, "People join companies and leave supervisors," and I really believe that. I think they get attracted to a company's culture and success, but if you have a bad manager out there, then people aren't going to put up with it and they'll leave. Find your bad managers and develop them or terminate them.

Training

We provide our new hires with six to eight weeks of training, which I believe gives them precise concepts of what is expected of them, how they can be successful and who their role models are. It develops loyalty and immediately sets company culture for them. Our training is designed to make people successful. You learn how to build customer loyalty and how to help your customer solve business problems. This all ties back to having a sense of accomplishment in what you do and when you have that feeling who would want to leave.

Benefits and Compensation

Just because a company offers one healthcare plan over another it will not build loyalty. I think that it's all part of the culture that the company develops. The company should have a good program that watches out for people and shares responsibility with them. It's an overall piece of the total package. However, if a company doesn't have the right management or the right company direction, the best benefits package in the country will not foster loyalty.

Similarly, compensation is important to a certain point. In the long-term, other factors such as environment and opportunities may have a stronger effect, but pay is undeniably a motivator to a certain point. You have to pay people correctly to get them in the right mind set. People want to feel comfortable with what they're making and the value that they are adding. After that, they're going to look for, challenging work, good supervisors and growth development path. However, there is a threshold point where the motivation is no longer just the money, but the challenge of the job and the work environment that you create.

Reviews

Reviews are another communication vehicle and they should be used as a chance and an opportunity to coach for better performance. I think people shy away from giving good, solid, constructive feedback because managers have a hard time sharing that information and feel uncomfortable doing it. They need to learn how to do those assessments because they offer an opportunity for the manager and a subordinate to sit down and talk. These meetings shouldn't be done once a year; they should be part of an ongoing communication throughout the whole year. That builds loyalty because it makes somebody say, "I have a person who cares for me."

People like to know how they are doing and how they can improve. If management can honestly tell employees those two things, then they help create an environment in which people can grow and improve.

Department Teamwork

Everybody wants to feel as though they are part of the success, but I think departments get very busy from time to time and don't share their successes. Departments need to communicate. They need to take time to get together and talk about problems, victories and upcoming issues. I think that builds a teamwork bond because the employees are in the know and understand what's going on in their particular areas.

Off-sites work, but I think sometimes they're overplayed. Everybody likes to go off and have a couple of days for strategic planning, but I think the real test of is whether the strategies developed at the off-site are actually applied in the workplace.

Remote Employees

As people work remotely, fostering loyalty becomes more difficult. It is difficult to make people feel they are part of something bigger than themselves when they have no social interaction. People need that human touch.

If you don't have that social aspect of work, that team-building, that peer relationship, it creates challenges that I think, as we create more of these virtual workforces, we have to strongly consider. We still need to have good management, measurement systems and face-to-face meetings. People in work environments need to feel part of something bigger then just themselves.

Measuring Loyalty

You can measure employee loyalty by looking at your turnover rates and whether or not they are below industry standard. I think you can also look at it by your ability to attract new people through, for example, college recruiting. If you've created that employment brand, that loyalty factor, people talk. If you have a good college relations program that lines people up to come to you, something's working right on that loyalty program that you have. If your referral rates go up year after year, you are doing something right. You can also measure loyalty by stock value. If the stock price goes up, you probably have a stable workforce that is driving value for your company without a lot of turnover.

You measure employee happiness and loyalty by turnover, employee referral rates, increased company sales, growth in the company and growth in share value. Those are all of the things on which you try to put an ROI to show that you are creating an employment brand and therefore a loyalty brand that has value to the company.

Brad Mousseau has spent over 25 years working in human resources. During that time he gained valuable experience in the high tech field. Over the course of his career he has worked at Wang Laboratories, Inc. Centocor, Inc., Gabrielli Medical Information systems, Systems and Computer Technologies, PC Connection, Inc. Mr. Mousseau received his B.A. from Keene State College and his M.B.A. from Rivier College.

Influencing Finances and Adding Value in HR

Brett Cohen

Senior Vice President, Human Resources
AmeriCredit

Leadership Goals

The ultimate goal of my position is to enable the work force to execute the company's strategy. To do that, the human resources function must continually focus on shifting the performance curve in a positive direction. You want to obtain the best results from any dollars the company spends on its people. In some companies, roughly 70 percent of the operating expense is related to people.

The first way for human resources to add value for the company is to promote a consumer-driven perspective of managing health care cost throughout the company. That is the single largest line item in the HR budget that is fairly controllable. We spend about $20 million on healthcare costs. If people can begin to spend the money like it is their own, it will make a huge difference in the way those dollars are spent.

The next biggest area of direct impact is in building a line of sight between the organization's goals and individual performance. This can be done by means of a performance management and incentive compensation process. In any organization, you get what you pay for. We are trying to create incentive programs that are very clearly linked to our business objectives. This ensures that people are focused on the right things, and we have already seen evidence that the programs are yielding very positive results.

The third and most significant way that the human resources function can affect the financial performance of the organization is somewhat indirect. It stems from the leadership development initiatives that enhance the organization's leadership bench strength. We perform talent reviews to identify the future leaders of the business, and provide development opportunities to all employees to enhance the overall level of talent throughout the organization. Although it can be difficult to put a dollar value on the impact of our leadership development initiatives, the executive team recognizes the critical role that leadership plays in the success of our company.

Retention efforts have also significantly impacted the bottom line. There are great costs involved in bringing someone onboard and training that person. To spend that time and effort only to have them leave the company soon after becomes an expensive hobby. If you can somehow reduce turnover, there are great benefits for the company. When we have given the area due attention, we have had some success in reducing those turnover levels. The trick is to target your retention efforts towards the high performing segment of your empbyee population because some types of turnover can actually be advantageous to the organization (e.g. poor performers).

The Art of Human Resources

The art of human resources lies in the ability to become entirely transparent to the organization. It is reaching the point when every manager in the company acts like an HR manager, without even realizing it. For example, if my team developed structured interviews for a position and the manager started using them, she would ultimately see a better caliber of hired employees. The manager may take the credit for hiring more qualified people, and that would be fine. It does not matter how it occurred. We want only to ensure that management has the tools and techniques that aid in the process. Once that has been done, they can take ownership of those methods because they are the people putting them into action. They are on the front lines interacting with their employees. It is almost impossible for HR to have a great impact unless we succeed in transferring our skills to those on the front line.

The Qualities of a Successful HR Executive

The primary quality of a successful HR executive is excellent leadership. At the same time, things are accomplished through a team. I will not have the expert knowledge in compensation that my compensation specialist will possess. I am not as skilled at leadership development as my leadership development person will be. You must hire good talent and obtain the best work from them at all times. The HR world is a broad arena. You must hire people who will keep in touch with that fact and then make sure they do their best.

Secondly, an HR executive needs the ability to think strategically. Your view of the organization must encompass the big picture. You must be able to think and talk like an executive in operations. That is the only way to win credibility. It is not enough to toss out HR terms and focus only on those issues. You need to possess an understanding of what drives the business.

An HR executive must have financial acumen. Since our operating expenses are about 70 percent people costs, we have to understand what takes place within those expenses in order to manage them. It is the only way to minimize expenses and maximize the investment. Lastly, an HR executive has to have a keen business perspective, the courage to stand up for what is right, and the credibility to make others listen.

Strategies for Success

The best strategy an HR executive can adopt in the workplace is to remember to simplify. No matter how complex the concept or product, the version that reaches the customer has to be simplified. Some people in the field of HR prefer to use HR jargon. The people on the line are not interested in what it is called. A message that is simpler becomes transferable and can be owned by someone outside of HR. I use a simple acronym called the human resources DREAM Team to highlight the five areas where HR can drive success. The critical areas are to develop, retain, engage, attract, and measure talent. If you can focus on those five, you will be successful within your organization.

Executing the basics exceptionally well helps to build credibility when delving into more of the value-added activities. If someone calls with a benefits question, you must be able to answer it. That is not necessarily the value-add aspect of your department, but unless you can show that it can be done perfectly well, you will not be allowed to play in the value-added arenas.

Also, partnering closely with the finance department to minimize spending on HR expense items and maximize spending on HR investment items. If you can attain credibility with the finance group, they will let you participate in new and different areas. So as an example, I will not spend frivolously by trying to hold my training classes in a world-class facility if it will cost the company a fortune. If I can demonstrate that HR will be fiscally responsible and dedicated to keeping our expenses in check, it provides us with the credibility needed to obtain funding for the truly important investments like our leadership development initiatives and incentive compensation programs.

Overcoming Human Resources Challenges

One of the most emotional challenges of human resources is conducting a mass reduction in force. To handle that, you must treat the individual with as much dignity as possible. A generous severance package can also help to soften the blow, but that will always be a traumatic experience. Aside from those aspects, every other challenge I have experienced in the HR arena has been fun and exciting. Even an event like a downsizing can have a positive outcome if it is handled correctly. For example, when HR went through a significant reduction in force here a couple of years ago, we centralized a lot of the administrative functions and created an HR call center. The immediate result was actually an improvement in the level of customer service in handling HR questions. In addition, the elimination of a number of support positions in the field forced our HR managers to abandon their prior transactional roles, and freed them up to become strategic business partners within their business units.

Working with Other Company Executives

As the head HR executive, I work most closely with legal, finance, and operations executives. I must understand each of their general perspectives in order to frame discussions with them in a successful manner. If you meet with the COO to sell him on an HR program, you will fail if you have not taken into account the potential disruption of the rollout on their operation or the timing in terms of their peak production requirements. Lacking that kind of understanding in advance will diminish your credibility very quickly.

As an example, because we have a monthly incentive program in our collection centers, people tend to crunch a lot of work into the end of the month. If we attempted to roll out a program at the end of month, it would be a terrible idea that would leave people very unhappy. Understanding the different needs of the functional areas helps you avoid those traps. The same thinking applies if dealing with the CFO. You should always be able to back up what you are discussing.

Assembling an HR Team

When I select a member of the team, I look for the same skills that are needed for my position. A new hire will essentially be groomed to do what I do, so they will need the same abilities. A member of the HR team will need to have excellent leadership, strategic thinking, and financial acumen in order to succeed. He or she will also need a developed business perspective and the courage to do what is right and stand up for their choices. Lastly, they will need to have technical expertise in their particular area.

I do not set goals for my team. I align my own objectives with the corporate strategy and then share those with the team. They set their goals according to that information. An automated performance management system is used to check on the progress of goals. Those systems are directly linked to the salary planning system. This connection motivates employees to achieve goals, because they are aware of the impact on their own bottom line. That is, essentially, our checks and balances system. Team members want to achieve their goals because they are paid on the basis of that achievement, and they can also see the importance of what they are achieving, since their personal goals are aligned with the corporate goals.

A Changing Approach to HR

The approach to human resources has gone through some changes in the past few years. The widespread availability of reliable and effective outsource providers has made it much easier to minimize the transactional components of human resources. This frees us to place more focus on the strategic initiatives. It also allows us to spend more time partnering with operations to proactively address their performance issues. Outsourcing has enabled us to be much more strategic. Because HR is more strategically focused, this has caused a slight shift from a profession of employee advocate to one of a business leader who will more objectively determine what is best for the business.

In the future, human resources will splinter into two factions. One will focus on the transactional aspect of HR, and the other will focus on the strategic aspect. They will likely be very separate and parallel tracks, with little overlap between the two professions. It is rare to find an HR professional who does well at both of those components.

Also, because vendors can provide most of the technical human resources processes at a reasonable cost, it is likely that companies will shift the remaining responsibilities to line managers. This may ultimately lead to the demise of generalist roles. As more and more questions can be answered from a service center or outsourced provider, it will not be necessary to have an HR person on-site to help with those problems.

The Three Golden Rules of Human Resources

Understand the business.

Understand the internal customers' needs and perspectives.

Always execute exceptionally.

Letting Someone Go

Early Warning Signs

We have had some success in discovering potential concerns by using 90-day performance review periods after someone is hired. During the first 90 days, we put gates in where we evaluate their performance, attendance and how they are doing. Results can appear very early. Since we use external recruiters, it allows us to evaluate our hires. There is a fee for each hire, and we have negotiated a strategy with the recruiter wherein our fee cost is reduced if the person leaves within a certain period of time. If people are not working well, we are aware of that fairly quickly.

There are some specific warning signs and red flags. Attitude will appear very early if it is going to be a problem. Attendance issues should be something to note. If car trouble and other little issues continue to arise, that kind of behavior can be an early indicator of future problems.

Trying to Correct the Problem

The essential steps usually begin with a verbal warning. If someone slides off track initially, they are usually told what is being done wrong. If that does not work and they are still making the same mistakes or the problem still exists, it may be necessary to advance to a written warning. Then there might be one more corrective warning before termination.

The manager is accountable for monitoring the situation. They must simply remain attentive in order to detect whether things have improved. It is their job to manage the people. If the work force is well trained and the managers in the field know what they are doing, it should not be necessary to involve Human Resources until the termination phase. This would be a check to see that everything has been documented appropriately and procedures have been followed correctly. It requires managers to be trained and up to speed so that they can work legally and effectively.

Most companies have multiple-step processes. The specific expectations are written out, including the timeframes and the consequences of failing to follow the instructions. Necessary elements of the process depend on what the particular issue is. Generally, it is important to focus on the actual behaviors and what can be done to improve them, rather than focusing on characteristics of the individual. What should be noted is how their behavior affects job performance and not any character or personality flaws.

Common Pitfalls During Dismissal

Certainly one of the most common pitfalls when dismissing an employee is not documenting everything adequately. That is probably the most frequent problem. A manager may come to you and announce that they are ready to terminate a person, but when asked what that employee did there is absolutely no documentation. Other pitfalls are often encountered when trying to terminate someone on employee leave. It can be difficult to try to terminate someone in that situation.

Therefore, understanding all of the legislation regarding FMLA, ADA and the various leave policies is extremely crucial. For example on FMLA, someone can be out for up to twelve weeks on unpaid leave if they meet the eligibility requirements. But sometimes the reason they were out on leave could also qualify them for consideration under the Americans with Disabilities Act. Knowing exactly how all of those leaves are related is very important, because sometimes it can be difficult or cause problems. Many issues can be overcome simply by being familiar with the regulations. When making those kinds of decisions, you most likely do want to involve HR and the legal department. Usually, that is where the expertise is going to be.

The last pitfall would be not terminating someone fast enough once they have become a problem. Sometimes people can simply hold on too long. They may miss an opportunity to terminate someone, and then they find themselves wanting to give the person another chance, even after they have repeatedly demonstrated problems. That kind of situation can develop into even larger problems, all of which could have been prevented earlier.

Wrongs Against the Company and Rapid Dismissal

If an employee commits a wrong against the company, you must first understand all of the circumstances by doing an investigation. Ultimately, if it is a conduct violation or another issue that is clearly unacceptable, the immediate result will be termination of employment. If it is a clear-cut issue, it will be signed off on fairly quickly, so finding a system for termination is not really a problem when the issue is severe.

In the event of a rapid dismissal, you want to capture what the events were if at all possible. If any questions arise, you should be sure to talk to the appropriate people and find answers. Sometimes it may be useful to give someone a decision-making leave, in which they are notified of a paid suspension for twenty-four hours. The employee will be told to go home because an investigation must be conducted. That would be one way of getting that person out of the work setting in order to do due diligence before termination.

Layoffs

A typical compensation for employees who are laid off is one to two weeks per year of service. However, we have taken a different approach. We provide four weeks per year of service for employees up to the officers' level, and six weeks per year of service for those who are officers or above. That compensation is far above the norm, but it has a number of advantages. First, we have found that we encounter virtually no lawsuits. Because the system has reduced the potential for hassles in litigation on the backend, it has been worthwhile. Another benefit is that the individuals who were separated from the company feel that they were treated fairly. As a result, when we started growing the business again, we found that it was fairly easy to attract our previously separated employees back to the company.

New Legislation

Some of the most recent employment legislation that has taken place has involved changes in FLSA, which affect who is classified as exempt or nonexempt. Other than that, there does not seem to be any recent or pending employment legislation that is significant. However, the changes in the way that stock options are expensed, and the new restrictions on deferred compensation plans are having a fairly significant impact on how companies are addressing their total rewards strategy.

Avoiding Potential Legal Issues

If a company is displeased with an employee but fears possible ramifications and legal issues, the best course of action is to document effectively and do a cost-benefit analysis. Ultimately, an employee who disrupts the workplace can do the most damage, and it may be wise to take any chances that could accompany terminating that person.

The same disciplinary processes that are used today have been used for decades, so I do not anticipate that there will be any radical changes in the marketplace. Treat the person fairly, document and give them every chance to improve. That is the acceptable way to proceed.

Certainly in the process of restructuring, it is possible for a firing to end on good terms. It is much easier in a situation like a layoff, because the employee knows that there are business reasons behind the decision. If the termination is because of performance it can be handled with dignity, but it is generally an unpleasant experience.

e-Learning Applications

The Benefits of E-Learning Programs

The ability to deliver training to geographically dispersed locations is very valuable. In addition, e-learning programs offer value in the ability to administer something in a very standardized fashion. E-learning can therefore be very useful in providing compliance training, where the accuracy of the information provided is critical. It helps to know that everyone is receiving the same message in the same way. The programs also provide benefits in time. People can take them when it is convenient.

E-learning programs can certainly impact a company's bottom line by reducing expenses. If you have the right programs, in some cases they can be done more cost-effectively with e-learning. Also certain programs, such as sales training, have the potential to enhance revenue as well. It provides the ability to teach employees the skills so that they can turn around and immediately generate improved volume. That type of program directly impacts the bottom line.

Targeting the technology side of a business can make a lot of sense. If you are learning how to program in a new language and you learn it on an e-learning program, you will be learning it in the same modality it will later be applied in. This provides an easy transfer of learning, which makes a lot of sense. Also, to the extent that you define marketing and sales as one realm, sales training initiatives can be very valuable when taught with e-learning programs.

The teaching tools can apply to office administration as well. In many software programs such as Word or PowerPoint, doing an e-learning program will be virtually identical to using the actual tool. That can be a big benefit of using those tools. The expense of e-learning programs depends on the program, but generally, they are very cost-effective.

What to Know Before You Sign

When signing on to adopt an e-learning program, be sure that you know the requirements and the costs associated with any modifications to the program. Know whether there will be new versions or releases in the future. The basic need is to understand all of the hidden costs associated with it. You will also want to collect bids from a number of different vendors, since the costs can vary significantly from one vendor to another.

When determining the length of the e-learning program, a shorter length is always better. People have short attention spans when it comes to e-learning. We try to keep our modules to ten or fifteen minutes at the most. Also as far as support, it is useful to have a help line number that the employee can call during the program.

New Developments

Aside from e-learning, we have had much recent success with action learning teams. We pull together high-potential managers from different functions and give them a business problem to work on. They work on it for a period of three to six months, and then the group delivers the results to the organization. We have realized a number of benefits from this team method. It helps to break down the silos across our various departments, and provides our executive team with more exposure to the early career talent within the organization.

In the next year, e-learning may shift so that companies will rely less and less on their internal systems to host the content. There are a number of vendors that allow you to purchase the content from them, but they will host it online. You do not have to worry about building any of the infrastructures in your own company. It is a method that makes a lot of sense, and it will probably increase in popularity in the near future.

Brett Cohen has seventeen years of human resources experience, including ten years at Verizon, and the past four and a half years at AmeriCredit. Mr. Cohen earned a bachelor's in Psychology from the University of Arizona, and a Master's in Industrial/Organizational Psychology from Texas A&M University (and another 4 years or so at the University of South Florida working on a never completed PhD.)

Business Transformation of Learning

Nick van Dam

Global Chief Learning Officer
Deloitte Touche Tohmatsu

Deloitte is an organization of member firms devoted to excellence in providing professional services and advice. We are focused on client service through a global strategy executed locally in nearly 150 countries. With access to the deep intellectual capital of 120,000 people worldwide, our member firms (including their affiliates) deliver services in four professional areas: audit, tax, consulting, and financial advisory services. Our member firms serve over one-half of the world's largest companies as well as large national enterprises, public institutions, and successful, fast-growing global growth companies.

We are ultimately in the business of *intellectual capital,* as our people are our *products.* Providing our practitioners with the expertise, best practices and capabilities to build new skills is incredibly important in this highly knowledge intensive industry. My role is two-fold in the Firm, and I find that this enables and energizes a perspective that drives a strong, strategic business focus for our global learning initiatives.

Approximately 70% of my work is targeted internally as the Global Chief Learning Officer. This internal Global HR learning role involves building best-of-breed learning capabilities for Deloitte that are cost competitive and that provide our people with the learning they need in order to successfully serve our clients around the world.

The other 30% of my time is employed as a Global Director in our Change, Learning and Leadership Practice. In this practice, I advise clients on the creation of business value through the business transformation of their learning function, and on implementation of effective human resources development (HRD) strategies. Furthermore, I contribute to the thought leadership and eminence in the Firm through speaking engagements and published books and articles.

The Financial Benefits of Global Learning Capabilities

A major component of our learning portfolio is comprised of e-learning programs and solutions that we make available within Deloitte on a global basis. For example, our people around the world have access to 4,000+ e-learning programs; 6,200 online books; online learning curricula; in addition to online self-service solutions for creating individual learning plans.

These globally consistent and accessible learning capabilities have a valuable financial benefit to the Firm on several levels.

- First, by providing our people with just-in-time, personalized learning, people's knowledge and skills are enhanced, driving individual and business performance.
- Secondly, it allows us to train our people on a more consistent global basis, supporting overall quality and risk management goals.
- Third, it decreases the overall time to market for new skills. Particularly, in fast growing practices such as China and India, it is important that our people have quick access to all new methodologies, leadership programs, and systems training, for example.
- Finally, it is our objective to provide our people with access to more learning programs and solutions at reduced costs. Offering these learning opportunities will help us to attract, redeploy and retain people. This limits our employee turnover, and helps our people to continue to grow professionally.

Success in Human Resources

The key to successful HR is adding value as a business partner by translating business strategies into people strategies.

Key capabilities to fulfill this HR responsibility in the global environment include:
- Partnership with business leadership
- Setting priorities in the midst of complexity
- Embracing cultural diversity
- Leading change
- Continuous mastery of new insights and ideas
- Motivating high performance teamwork and achievement
- Measuring the business impact of HR initiatives

The main mission of an HR function is to support the business by defining HR initiatives which are aligned with the business goals and supported by business leadership. Therefore, HR executives must master and maintain a deep understanding of the business and be very well connected with the business leaders. My work in our Human Capital practice keeps me close to the important business issues that companies and organizations grapple with daily and helps me to ensure that our HRD initiatives are aligned closely with real business concerns.

Although intuitively all recognize the important link between the business and HR as important, it remains very difficult for many HR professionals to accomplish. Most businesses today are large, complex, global, matrixed organizations. As a result – HR Leaders may find themselves interfacing simultaneously with many of business leaders complicating the prioritization of HR initiatives. HR programs cannot be dictated from the top. Therefore, it is important that HR leaders work concurrently with multiple business leaders and other HR leaders on all levels to get buy-in and support for the prioritization of initiatives. Especially in a professional services firm like Deloitte, building consensus around new ideas and approaches relies on building networks of strong personal relationships and leveraging the networks to foster alignment around a vision.

Another key competency required of HR leaders is the ability to effectively communicate with these multiple constituencies. In a global organization it is important that HR executives in regional and global roles have a mindset that embraces the variety of cultures of the people with whom they work. As mentioned before, at Deloitte we have about 120,000 people within 150 countries. In order to successfully implement initiatives on a global basis, we must work them through the business cultures of various countries. This is a daunting challenge, but without undertaking this effort, no initiative can be globally effective. It is the true expression of *Think Globally, Act Locally*, albeit with the global HR leader being on the forefront of both perspectives.

In addition, HR executives must be fast learners capable of leading major change. HR executives must keep focused on internal and external environmental impacts that influence their business and industry, proposing HRD solutions that support mastery of new knowledge and skills. They must ensure that their networks of peers and colleagues constantly reinvigorate their understanding of the context for their own strategy. In addition, new HR approaches must be recognized and managed as major change initiatives and that all the steps for leading major change are considered and implemented.

Effective team management is also a core skill for HR executives. They need to attract the right people to HR and understand how to motivate them. First and foremost they must define the roles and competencies needed for their HR team, while motivating and measuring performance against specific goals and objectives that are clearly defined and inspiring to the members of the team. One of the keys to motivation is to allow significant individual leverage and decision-making to achieve the goals, keeping a close watch that the target is met or exceeded.

Another important key to success in an HR leadership role is to implement initiatives which have a measurable impact on the business. At Deloitte we have embraced a Balanced Scorecard approach to metrics that can be influenced by HR initiatives, such as measuring Turnover of Talent and percentage of Woman in Leadership roles, among others.

The Role of HR within the Organization

As an HR executive, I work with the organizational, functional and country business leaders in the four lines of our business: audit, consulting, financial advisory services and tax. I also collaborate with my colleagues in other HR roles. My specific focus area is learning, which involves working with all of the professionals in education or learning roles the 150 countries where we have practices.

The complexity of designing a global learning function that supports business objectives, embraces cultural diversity, and engages our practitioners from all functions, industries, and regions, is enormous. It requires a highly integrated global team of specialists who create and deliver learning initiatives in coordination with the regional and country learning professionals.

Over the years, the requirements have lead to the development of a global team comprised of several communities of expertise:
- business leadership liaison
- design and development

- technology infrastructure
- communication, marketing and customer care

For example, one team interfaces with business leaders to identify and discuss specific learning needs and then prioritizes learning initiatives. Another group is responsible for design of programs, such as our Leadership Programs, and these professionals must both understand our businesses, as well as the core competencies required of our leadership to achieve our business objectives. Furthermore, they need to understand how to design effective learning programs for senior executives. To support our cutting-edge learning infrastructure, there is a technology team which ensures that the on-line learning is reliable, accessible and trackable.

I also have people on my team who have a strong background in communications and marketing, who support and market all learning initiatives in the countries. This is integral to ensuring that all in our global practice know about our learning capabilities. In addition, a number of global learning initiatives are lead by learning country-located professionals who are so called 'double-headed'. They might be responsible for both learning in a country and also lead a global initiative. One of the key benefits of this approach is that it brings a country perspective to the forefront and additionally provides excellent insights regarding the best way to implement an initiative.

On a continual basis, the business leadership around the world and I discuss the goals for the overall global learning function in addition to my personal goals. Annually, I give very detailed and specific goals to the people who report to me. These goals are defined with both qualitative and quantitative measures, so that we can evaluate our progress at a mid-year review and then adjust them for the remainder of the year.

The Changing Focus of HR

Economic, social and technological forces continue to change the global economy and enterprises around the world. Companies are forced to build competitive advantage with a focus on operational excellence, customer intimacy and/or market leadership. As companies are becoming more knowledge intensive and focus on services, there is an increasing focus on a high performance workforce. Thus, the role of Human Resources is rapidly emerging from a traditional administrative transactional role to a strategic role. In this new role, HR partners with the business to build organizational capabilities that have a direct impact on the bottom line.

For example, HR can make the concept of employee self-service a reality while supporting the business objective of operational excellence. Employee self-service can include areas such as: learning and development, compensation and benefits, performance management, coaching, and recruitment, among others. The HR function must work with both internal and external partners to build the capabilities and infrastructure necessary to execute this strategy—a highly complex and difficult task, but one that is expected by workers in the 21st century.

Anther critical focus for HR is strategic talent management. By 2008, a wealth of skills and experience will begin to disappear from the market as the first members of the Baby Boom generation turn 62. For example, it is expected that in automotive manufacturing, up to 40% of managers will be eligible to retire within the next five years. The US public sector could loose more than a third of their government employees by 2010. As more people retire, the shortage of talent grows. The Hudson Institute (2004) finds that only 20% of today's workforce has the skills for 60% of the jobs in the year 2020. This has significant implications for sourcing of talent and the need for intensive training and development capabilities in enterprises.

The Business Potential of e-Learning

From a business impact perspective, there are three categories where e-learning programs can add significant value. First, it can improve company earnings by reducing the overall learning costs. Research data has shown that enterprises can save between 30% - 70% in their overall learning expenses by moving towards a just-in-time and online learning model. Secondly, e-learning can enhance workforce productivity by reducing the training time, by decreasing the time-to-competence and/or by enhancing the knowledge base and skills of people. A third area in which e-learning can add value is by enhancing company revenue. A growing number of companies sell e-learning programs to their customers, partners and suppliers and are therefore able to generate revenue.

e-Learning programs can support a number of specific business goals. For example, the launch of many new products and services requires training for different groups of people, such as sales force, customer service, and help desk workers. Leveraging e-learning ensures courses are instantly available around the world, thereby increasing the speed-to-market of new products and services. e-Learning can also support a faster deployment of new information systems and business processes. In addition, compliance training has emerged as the number one e-learning program category for many companies. This is driven primarily by legal and regulatory mandates.

e-Learning programs can provide a globally consistent and lower-cost orientation program for new hires. Additionally, a sales force benefits tremendously from just-in-time training that can be taken from any location at any time, supporting the business needs to spend as much as time in the market with customers as possible. e-Learning has also proven to be very powerful in providing access for leadership to immediate learning. Finally, e-learning can extend learning to customers, partners and suppliers, building supporting linkages and commitment in the value chain.

Interestingly, the e-learning model has proven to be very effective in emerging markets such as China and India, with China being the fastest growing country for e-learning in the Asia/Pacific region, according to IDC (2004).

Global enterprises are expanding headcount rapidly in these countries, and it is critical to familiarize new employees with their new employer including: culture, organization, business process, products and services, and information systems. The sheer numbers of new hires combined with the logistical and cost challenges of traditional classroom learning models deliver costly and slow on-boarding results. Employing an e-learning strategy to on-board new hires at Deloitte, we find that consistent messages about the Firm and our culture, processes, services and systems, can be rolled out quickly and cost-effectively as people are hired. In addition, we find that employees in China and India are highly motivated to take e-learning, as it supports their personal goals to enhance individual skill sets and progress faster in their careers.

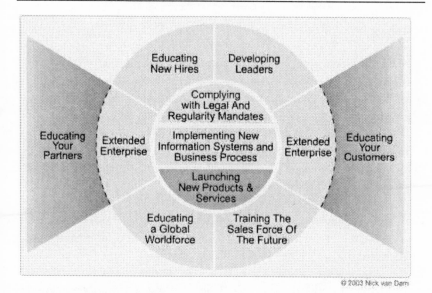

© 2003 Nick van Dam

e-Learning Market Trends

From an overall adoption perspective, the e-learning market will continue to grow over the next years. The market for e-learning did not exist until 1996 and grew close to $8 billion dollars in 2004. IDC (2004) predicts that the e-learning market will be up to $21 billion by 2008. It is clear that global adoption of e-learning will continue to increase significantly as this trend moves forward.

Figure 1: Worldwide Corporate e-Learning by Region, 2004 and 2008 ($M)

	2004	2008
Americas	5,667	15,154
EMEA	1,235	3,572
Asia/Pacific	1,084	2,396
Total	7,986	21,122

Source: IDC, 2004

e-Learning trends to watch include:

Learning business processes will be automated and more employees will have access to self-service learning capabilities. This includes functionality to develop online learning plans which support enhancements in workforce performance.

E-learning vendors will expand their off-the-shelf learning portfolios, and there will be a great variety of learning courses for different industries, competence areas, available in multiple languages.

From an e-learning design and courseware perspective, there are a number of new trends developing. First, e-learning will become more and more sophisticated and of higher quality. Much has been learned about how people best learn in an e-learning environment and significant improvements in related instructional design. I foresee an exponential increase in the quality of e-learning courseware. Secondly, we are moving to more stimulation-based learning because this mirrors the real work environment. Additionally, game-based learning will emerge as important type of e-learning, as it is very engaging and is familiar to the Internet generation who will join enterprises in the coming years. Finally, more e-learning content will be designed for deployment in smaller learning objects and e-learning modalities, such as: online books; job-aids; mini-courses; online self-study guides; and, audiobooks, among others.

Moving forward, more e-learning will be deployed on a wide range of hardware devices including: computers, PDAs, MP3 players and mobile phones, providing people with any-time and any-place access to learning.

Online learning portals and knowledge management portals will be consolidated into one portal that will provide *one-stop* access for people to acquire knowledge and learning.

Finally, the adoption of e-learning will increase even more rapidly as new hires emerge from college, already as heavy Internet users, and expect that their employers will provide online learning experiences to build knowledge and skills.

Nick van Dam, is author of The e-Learning Fieldbook, McGraw-Hill, 2004 (www.elearningfieldbook.com) which presents business case studies and lessons learned by 25 leading companies. He is the founder of e-Learning for Kids, a non-profit organization that provide children and schools with internet based training at not costs. (www.e-learningforkids.org)

Mr. van Dam is the Global Chief Learning Officer for Deloitte Touche Tohmatsu and Global Director in Deloitte's Change, Learning, and Leadership Practice. He has held a variety of global Learning and Human Resources Development (HRD) leadership roles throughout his career in several different countries. Most recently, he led the transformation of Deloitte's Learning organization, an effort that received much award recognition.

As an internationally recognized consultant and thought leader in Learning and HRD, Mr. van Dam has written articles and has been quoted by The Financial Times, Forbes, Fortune, Business Week, Management Consulting, Learning & Training Innovations Magazine, T+D Magazine, Bizz Magazine, The India Times, and others. He is a columnist for CLO Magazine and Intellectueel Kapitaal (IK) Magazine. He has also authored and co-authored a number of books and articles. His most recent publication, The e-Learning Fieldbook (McGraw-Hill), presents business case studies and lessons learned by twenty-five leading companies.

Journey to Employer of Choice

Jon C. Cecil
Chief Human Resources Officer
Lee Memorial Health System

79

Strategic Goals

Lee Memorial Health System is a public health care organization with no tax support and has over 6,000 employees and fifty locations with five acute care hospitals at three locations, and a number of other businesses in post-acute care, physician practices, and ambulatory and diagnostic centers. I have the privilege to serve as its Chief Human Resources Officer.

Since I'm at the Officer level (sometimes referred to as the "O" or "C" level), I tend to be more focused on our organization's mission and vision achieved through the accomplishment of our five strategic goals. One of these five strategic goals is our People goal, which is my personal area of focus.

Achieving our People strategic goal is essential for us to provide quality patient care and achieving our other four strategic goals. We have a very simple purpose statement for this strategy, which is to be an "Excellent Health Care Employer".

From our People strategic plan, we state, "Our ability to provide service and quality is dependent upon the people who deliver care or support its delivery. Our success, we measure through the use of employee satisfaction, attraction, and retention measures."

The plan's mission statement states, "To foster excellence in People practices through strengthening leadership, building high performance culture, redesigning work processes and jobs, improving human resource processes, and growing the next generation workforce." Most of everything that the Human Resources function does is built around this strategic plan.

Here are our five People Strategic Goals:

Strengthen Leadership
Strengthen leadership by building knowledge, focusing on accountability, building employee and volunteer trust, loyalty, engagement, and ensuring open communications.

Build a Diverse, High Performing Culture

Build a diverse culture that expects high performance, provides learning and personal development, fosters high employee and volunteer satisfaction, and rewards and recognizes excellence and ensures a safe workplace and promotes wellness and work/life balance

Continuously Improve Job Role/Process Design

Redesign work processes by identifying and eliminating non-value added activities to eliminate constraints to high performance; redesign jobs based on the redesigned work processes.

Continuously Improve Human Resource Processes

Ensure Human Resources processes are efficient and value added; demonstrate best practices, support retention, and recruitment, comply with rules and regulations, and maintain accreditation and licensure

Grow the Next Generation

Grow current and future workforce.

Setting specific goals and achieving the desired outcomes has led to financial success and viability of an organization. For example, our People plan targeted significant improvement in our retention and recruitment strategies. The establishment of a culture that invested in strengthening leadership and improving recruitment processes, resulted in substantial financial success for Lee Memorial, not to mention significant quality and customer service improvements. The ability use a balanced scorecard to cascade these 5 Health System Strategic goals (including the People strategy) all the way down to our front line staff and to align our performance incentives has been critical to improving organizational performance and achieving our goals in order to accomplish our mission and vision.

Successful HR

"Culture eats strategy for lunch", I didn't coin that phrase, but I often use it. And even though we have strategies to drive the organization, I believe the art of HR is being able to assist an organization identify and support the desired culture by building and strengthening its leadership to engage a workforce and help provide a dynamic and exciting work environment that celebrates successes and accomplishments.

To be successful, you certainly need an understanding of how to develop the right culture and leadership in your organization. Once you're moving in that direction, then you need to be able to establish appropriate goals and measurements (metrics) to monitor your progress and make course corrections as needed to achieve your stated outcomes.

Perhaps, not widely understood in other industries, health care may well be one of the most complex business environments in the world today. There is a broad array of jobs, job skills, and competencies needed for all levels in our health system that operates in a highly regulated and chaotic external environment.

For an example, we have over 700 job descriptions within our health system. Certainly, we could do better in reducing the number, but many of these jobs are legitimate and bona fide positions necessary for unique operations. Our workforce consists of the very top of the health care employment chain from neurosurgeons to clinicians to business/administrative jobs to entry level positions in warehousing/distribution, food production and housekeeping. This complexity of positions leads to a vary complex and comprehensive culture.

A critical process to assess your culture and measure the success of your organization is to establish a comprehensive HR metrics system. Another phrase I borrowed from Tom Olivo of Success Profiles, Inc., is "What gets measured gets done".

Through a talented staff in Human Resources, a report called our Key Internal Workforce Indicator Report, or the KIWI Report is produced and distributed to leadership quarterly. Its has a simple and colorful format with graphics and explanations that are designed assist leadership from the top to the front line supervisor to communicate to their staff the outcomes of our numerous workforce indicators. It is an expectation of leadership to routinely share this information with their employees.

An important strategic goal is to improve Human Resources processes, so we can help enable the organization to achieve its desired outcomes. For example, the selection processes we utilize have several assessment tools to assure we are selecting the right people to join our organization. We also assess regularly our organization's workplace climate. Annual employee satisfaction surveys are done, as well as monthly satisfaction surveys. We focus on management styles (we call them, the seven drivers), develop appropriate leadership interventions, and establish action plans to assure we deliver our survey slogan, "You talk, we listen, and things change". We consistently report out to the leadership and employees our continued improvements.

Challenges in HR

One of the accomplishments I'm very proud of our Human Resources team is we have been able to move our People strategy to the top of the organization and have it valued and supported by all of our senior leadership. As noted earlier, I do believe this is a key strategy for us is to be able to accomplish our goals and objectives of the organization.

I believe another thing that's very important to an organization (our CEO recognized a number of years ago) is the importance of having the human resource function at the top of the organization, at the O's table. It is important for Human Resources leaders to shed the old misperceptions of what HR should be doing. We're not the warm and fuzzy huggers, the transactional bureaucracy, or the policeman of policies and procedures. Our existence should not depend on these functions. Our job is to add value to our organizations by partnering with our operations to help them achieve their goals.

We most demonstrate to the operational leaders the return on investment for investing or reinvesting in our People strategies and Human Capital. Our ability to deliver this information is to have built a strong HR metrics, so strategies and their outcomes can be quantified. It's a very powerful way of demonstrating to that you need to have a return on investment for any type of capital expenditures in today's business environment.

A Cohesive Team

At Lee Memorial, we have Senior Leadership Council, which sits the five chief officers and CEO. We have no other CEOs, other than our one health system CEO, and we do not have a system Chief Operating Officer. The five of us are virtually the Chief Operating Officer(s) for the health system. Including myself, we have our Chief Financial Officer, our Chief Patient Care Officer (Chief Nurse Executive), and two Chief Medical Officers (MD's). Of the two Chief Medical Officers, one is responsible for ambulatory and strategic services, and the other is responsible for our quality and clinical services.

In 1999 and 2000, for the first time in the recent history of the Lee Memorial Health System, we had devastating financial losses. Our CEO needed to restructure the senior leadership into a cohesive, smaller self directed team to help turnaround the health system. In a little over one year, this team made a $20+ million financial turnaround while improving the quality of care and services. Having a common vision, certainly bonded the team into achieving its outcomes. Once this team became a team, the culture began to shift and leadership began to strengthen throughout the organization. I am also proud of the value this team place on its human assets.

As noted, our team is focused on assessments and outcomes for our People strategies. When you make decision to select a leader, it needs to be the right decision the first time. It's just too painful for the organization, and too painful for the individual that was selected, for it to be the wrong decision. We've developed broad, leadership success profiles in the organization. Then we built our leadership selection process around those profiles and select through a behavioral interviewing process. In addition to other selection criteria, all supervisors and above go through a rigorous psychological assessment by an external industrial psychologist to assure fit in our organization.

One of the critical HR transformations we made about a half a dozen years ago was to move HR from a transactional-based operation to a partnership and center of expertise to support our operating units in the health system. To do that, we needed a different set of skills and competencies for the HR staff. This doesn't mean that there are not still a number of rules and regulations and information-type activities (transactional activities), which have to be done in HR. Unfortunately, with so many laws and regulations, you have to be in compliance. But to add value to the organization, HR must help the selection of the right people, develop them, and retain the right people, while removing barriers and obstacles to the operational leaders, so they can achieve their goals.

We redesigned our HR function to meet today's operational needs. A new position, the HR Business Partner, was created. These two positions partner with their operating units, assess the units' needs in order to be able to achieve their strategies and goals, and assist in the implementation and execution of these strategies. The HR Business Partners are charged with to the responsibility to bring HR expertise to operating units to help them improve their People processes, transfer HR knowledge, and achieve desired outcomes.

Next, we realized we have to have a group of specialists or experts to stay focused on key HR functions. In the past, our specialists had become generalists, and they were good at a lot of things, but not necessarily experts in their area. We had to make certain that our specialists stayed focused on their areas of expertise. A Center of Expertise was created. However, to allow our HR Business Partners and Experts to succeed, we had to off load a large number of the transactional tasks.

For example, we have some extremely talented folks in compensation and benefits. It just didn't make sense for one of our specialists to be pulled off a critical project by a routine transactional request that could be better handled by a lower skill level. Let's say a benefits specialist received a phone call from an employee to update their number of dependants, while deeply involved in a financial analysis. Unfortunately in the old world, this often happened. The specialists would respond, be distracted and lose focus on the analysis and increased the opportunity for errors and continuity of thought. This caused variability to their planning process which led to errors. This was such an inefficient way of operating an HR function. It was very important, and I can't emphasize the importance enough, that redesigning the HR processes is critical for not only HR success, but for the success of the organization.

Setting Goals

Part of our People Strategic Plan was a goal "to become an Employer of Choice". After 3 years of focus on this goal, last year, Lee Memorial was recognized along with 11 organizations in the country for the Employer Choice® recognition from the Herman Group. To be announced in January 2005, Lee Memorial just received the 2005 "Premier Health Care Employer" recognition from the J. Walter Thompson Corporation.

When we were striving for the Employer of Choice® recognition, we knew we had to achieve all of our of our five People Strategic goals, if this vision was to be realized. We did a comprehensive strategic plan with the input of many of the Human Resources and Organizational Effectiveness' customers. We needed to know from our customers what services we were providing that added value to operations. In addition, any area that had a significant impact on the People function/processes, such as Safety, Legal, Finance, Information Technology, Employee Health, Occupational Health, Workers Compensation, Communications and Marketing, Lean/Sigma, etc. participated in the planning event and future planning. Once the input was receive, then group the prioritized the action plans to achieve the specific goals and objectives. With action plans prioritized and timelines established, then a management operating system using a project management approach set accountabilities and desired outcomes.

"Strengthening Leadership" was our first goal by design. Understanding that without this fundamental enabler, hopes of achieving the other goals were dismal. Our Learning and Performance function, today know as Organizational Effectiveness, set about to develop a comprehensive change management process, development of our emerging leadership and continued leadership development all the way up to senior most level of the organization. As many of the tools gained traction, we quickly realized the value of this goal. With a stronger leadership, we were able to begin tackling some of the most challenging cultural issues to begin our organizational transformation.

With Leadership goals being attained, we could start to build a diverse and high performing culture, our second goal. With accountability, as well as recognition and reward systems in place, we began to see a new, more vibrant culture emerge. We learned from previous failure at the turn of the millennium that we could not "cut our way to prosperity", and realized an engaged workforce believing we would re-invest in our human capital to produce an ROI was the only way to meet our Mission and Vision.

Our third goal is continuously improving job role and process redesign. In health care today, what we get paid for our services is flat or declining. Our labor expenses this year are probably going to increase at least 4.2 percent. Our medical supply expenses are may increase to 7 to 10 percent increases. In health care, your customers tell you what you are going to be paid for your services, e.g., government – Medicare/Medicaid, insurance plans, etc. Given our location in Southwest Florida and the demographics of our area, Medicare may well be one our best payers. We are receiving between a .8 to .9% increase from Medicare which represents well over 50% of our business and a 0% increase from Medicaid. As you can see, we have a crisis and will not be able to survive if we continue to do business they we are. Compounding this dilemma is the rapid growth of uninsured or underinsured patients, particularly since Lee Memorial is the regional safety net health system. Thus, our only way to survive is to become more efficient by eliminating waste out of our operating systems and drastically reducing variations in our processes.

Our net revenues are over $500 million. Our total charges are about $1.4 billion, and in health care we never come near receiving full payment, so it's not really a realistic representation of revenue. Last year, expenses were approximately. $490 million and capital expenditures alone were $65 million. Typical health care organizations today are operating on a 2 percent or less bottom line, which is a very small margin in most industries. So redesigning our work processes and eliminating waste is all that we have left if we wish to stay a viable entity and meet our mission and vision.

As noted, we wanted to make certain we re-designed work processes, identified and eliminated non-value-added activities, eliminated constraints to high performance, and redesigned jobs based on the redesigned work processes. We have heavily engaged in our organization what we call lean/sigma program and have implemented a performance improvement program call W.A.V. E. (Waste/Annihilated/Value/Enhanced). We used a unique organizational transformation tool called our "Discovery Charts", which were pictorial representations on a chart to train over 4000 employees on the basic principals of waste reduction and elimination. This program significantly improved the understanding of waste and engagement of the workforce with this critical strategy. Accountability for achieving waste reduction was set at all levels from the front line worker to senior leadership. Although we have a long way to go, we have charted our course and are steering in the right direction for our future survival and success.

Our fourth goal is to continuously improve human resource processes. As stated earlier, this goal assures our human resources processes are efficient and truly value added, they demonstrate best practices, support retention and recruitment, and of course, complies with the rules, regulations, and maintains accreditation (quality certification). We can't do business the way HR has been done in the past. Our processes need to be as efficient or more efficient than any other processes in the health care system. This has been an arduous task with many pitfalls. Investment in new technology has helped, but HR is at the bottom of the Information Technology feeding chain for investment in a health care organization, where clinical technology rightfully reigns superior. We had to optimize the technology and be extremely creative and innovative with what tools we had. With a talented HR and IT team, much has been accomplished, and today, Lee Memorial is a "Best Practice" destination for many health care organizations and a few non-health care ones.

Lastly, is growing our next generation, which is growing our current and future workforce. This is a staggering problem for health care today. We're facing, in the next few years nationally, a 60,000 shortage in just RNs. We have a demand for RNs, and the colleges and universities have a supply of students want access, but they're not producing them. One would think colleges would salivate at an opportunity for a market place like this. Unfortunately, clinical programs are expensive to operate, and colleges and universities are facing funding reductions, also. We have worked for years with our local health care competitors to coordinate the development and growth of the health care workforce. In fact, we realigned our staffing within HR to create a position called "Strategic Workforce Planner." This individual analyzes our health system's workforce growth, identifies the gaps, and works within the organization and community to see that we our growing these future workers. We have invested part of our operating revenue to help fund grants and scholarships for our employees, fund new programs and faculty at the colleges and universities, and continue to present to primary and secondary schools the opportunity for a quality career in health care. We the emergence of the baby boomers as health care consumers, this problem will continue to rapidly escalate. I am astounded that the leadership in our government is not addressing the future crisis.

Using HR Metrics

Let's start with the macro approach. I am a born-again, diehard measure everything we do in HR. Just vision that you are starting your car in the morning, you look at your dashboard, your fuel tank's has a little orange light blinking, but you ignore that light. You drive down the road, and then you run out of gas and face the consequences of failing to heed the warning indicators. I have seen my own and other organizations either not have or know what the indicators are, or if they do have them, ignore the indicators. I believe a successful organization today must have useful and easy to access HR metrics or other measurements of their workforce.

One of the things we've spent a lot of time on over the last few years is making certain that we developed HR metrics, so that we can look at a dashboard to look. What I've seen in the past is we will get so involved and immersed in one issue, and we'll focus so much time and energy on it that we lose the big picture. To respond to this need, as noted, earlier the emergence of the KIWI report became a critical tool to assess where the greatest returns would be to invest HR and the organization's time on People goals.

Our goal is to make certain that we use the 80/20 rule; take the 20 percent of the high volume, high cost problems, and focus on these. The 80% will continued to be managed, but the 20% is where we will look at redesign, process improvement, or intervention. Let's not spend our resources on something that's not going to help us achieve our overall goals. We look for warning signs, like when that little orange light starts flashing on your fuel gauge. The KIWI report clearly identifies when one of our control charts are out of control and sends a signal to leadership to begin to take action

Taking Action on Employee Issues and Concerns

We have a very small, but viable employee relations function. By opening the communications and using our employee advocacy function, employees are able to alert leadership that we may have a problem, be it a process or leadership issue. We know with the complexity of human b eings, and 6,000 people, we're destined to have employees with problems. It's our responsibility in human resources to develop our managers and leaders to be able to deal with these and seek resolution.

What we don't want to do is to fabricate artificial management through HR. In other words, we should never take over the management of a department. If a leader or supervisor cannot effectively manage their employees, then we need to deal with that leader and correct the deficiencies, reassign, or move them out of the organization. As mentioned previously, Lee Memorial had a major organizational turnaround in 1999 and 2000. We had two years in the red losing$12 million. The following year after we made our turnaround effort, we when went from a $12 million loss a net gain from the previous year of $21 million. I am firmly convinced we did this by engaging our workforce and having leadership understand its role in employee engagement.

If we have a particular problem in the area, what I don't want HR to do, as we used to do in the past, is automatically assume that the manager or supervisor is wrong. I caution unless you get your facts, perceptions are exactly what they are, clearly perceptions. We need facts to make certain we understand reality. I think our employee relations specialists have become very skilled and very adept at quickly accessing the issues, slicing through many of the emotions, and focusing on the core issues with this particular employee.

Another thing we did was change our turnover metric, and said, "We really need to make certain that we're focused on controllable turnover". With this focus, we've become a best practice in voluntary turnover.

To give you an understanding of the importance of comprehensive measurement of outcomes. I was feeling pumped with our turnover outcomes and thought we might just be a best practice. Then I received information from the KIWI report that completely pulled the slats from underneath me. While our overall voluntary turnover was running below 8 percent, our turnover in employees in the first 12 months was 44 percent. Can you imagine the cost of that to the organization of hiring and replacing these people?

Realizing something had to be done, the HR team did considerable research to understand the issues and look for potential solutions. They quantified the cost of a proposed solution and presented their recommendations for senior leadership to fund. Cost savings were identified, which indicated a significant return on investment. Re-investment in our selection and attraction practices and a retention program for new hires was implemented. In the first year, a 13% reduction in new hire turnover was achieved through improved selection to assure we hired the right employee and an "On-Boarding Program" that provided workplace support for new employees.

If you spend the resources to select the right employee, you must make certain the work place they are entering is conducive for them being successful. The goal of the On-Boarding program was to provide a "buddy" system and support structure. When the new employee enters the workplace, they have a support person that is not a preceptor or their trainer, but a co-worker who is matched them to provide them a social entry. Now, they've somebody to go to lunch, talk, and just support them through the process. We recognize and reward our navigators by celebrating their successes. This program has not been that costly, has demonstrated its value, and received national recognition for its design and success.

To keep touch with the new employee, the On-Boarding Coordinator does sixty and one hundred twenty-day surveys with each one of our new hire employees. In addition, the coordinator is in touch with the assigned "buddy" or what we call the Navigator. If necessary, the coordinator will provide the work unit leader information or coaching to improve the new employee's conditions to help retain the new employee. Some areas are exceptional, and there is usually a direct correlation to low new hire turnover, whereas, units that do a poor job, turnover often is higher.

Sometimes the selection process fails. The employee is not the right fit in that department. The next question should be, "Is there somewhere else in the organization this person may fit better?" If not, then our goal is to make certain we get them out of our organization within the first ninety days. Otherwise, it just becomes more painful for everyone involved. Managers who aren't developed enough or strong enough to make these tough decisions to remove a person who do not fit, probably are not a fit in our organization.

We speak openly about Jim Collin's comments about getting the right people on the bus in the right seats or off the bus. Our leadership is expected to make certain that we've done all the right things by making the employee aware of their deficiencies, need for improvement of specific competencies, and assisted them to develop action plans for improvement. The supervisors must make this employee clearly aware of the consequences for not completing their action plans and when they do meet their action plans, celebrate the successes.

Firing Pitfalls and How to Overcome Them

You may hear a similar story from HR staff in other organizations. An HR generalist will receive a call from a supervisor as follows, "I got this horrible employee. Her name is Susan." Susan's been with us for ten years, and I know you (HR) are going to give me a hard time to get rid of her." In true fashion, the HR person will seek out Susan's personnel file and look at her past evaluations and documentation of performance. Guess what the HR person often finds? Her evaluation says that she is a great employee and "almost walks on water." There's nothing in her file letting the employee know of her performance issues or consequences for non-performance. With no documentation, no counseling, no coaching, the HR person recommends starting a formal process. The supervisor complains HR never will let them get this wrong person off the bus.

The patient HR person takes a deep breath, as they are trained and coaches and mentors the supervisor when they really want to say, "Are you kidding me?" HR works hard to minimize these types of scenarios because it will have to work backwards and do considerable rework or possibly face litigation. Regrettably, the HR person sometimes has to practice tough love and say to the supervisor, "No, I strongly recommend that we do not fire this employee. You have not done your job as a supervisor to be able to let Susan go." This response does not make the HR person one of the supervisor's favorite people.

At Lee Memorial, we've been very committed to a corrective action process versus a disciplinary process. This process has been in place for a number of years. When first started, some managers and directors said, "Our HR just doesn't want us to coddle poor employees." On the other hand, it is HR's responsibility to make certain that leaders are thoroughly educated and understands the value of the corrective action process, then holds leadership accountable for following the appropriate corrective action steps.

If you have the wrong fit for a person in a job, and you follow the appropriate and fair steps, you'll do the right thing for the employee, and you'll do the right thing for the organization. Considerable training is provided to leadership on coaching and mentoring. It's very, very important that each leader understands the value of each and every one of their employees and the significant cost of replacement. We want to make certain there's a fair and open dialogue with employees and their supervisors and the opportunity to correct deficiencies.

Let's say Susan is having a performance problem, and it's not due to attitude. The first expectation for the supervisor is to promptly, clearly, and directly address the issue with Susan. This is our coaching step. But Susan does not respond to the coaching and the performance problem is not resolved.

The next step is to identify educational processes that will help her minimize errors and improve performance. We call this the first step in the corrective action process—an oral warning and document.

The second step is initiated if Susan fails to improve her performance. There may be other complications, the communication was not clear, or next steps. Maybe Susan has a behavioral or attitude problem. Maybe she is facing an external crisis with her family or some serious situation. After all, she's been with the organization 10 years and has consistently had good evaluations. This step is called our written corrective action. The supervisor says to Susan, "Susan, we're serious about this. I will review with you again your deficiencies and you are required to bring us back an action plan of what steps you're going to take to correct this performance. And I'll sit down and help you with planning these steps if you like." This next step the supervisor is saying, "This is very serious and the consequences for failing to meet our agreed-upon action steps are further corrective action up to and including termination."

If Susan does not achieve her action plans, the decision-making leave step is initiated. The supervisor will say, "Susan, you're still not performing, ; you're not doing what you told me you were going to do, and this has become very serious. We are sending you home to reflect on your performance and improve your action plan.", so you can achieve it. I will pay you for half the day to work on your plans. The other half of the day you will not be paid, and you should use this time to think if you wish to continue your career with Lee Memorial. And while you're home for that half day, we're going to ask you to develop an action plan. We've already told you all the things that you need to do. Now we want to make certain that you understand what those things are, and we're going to make certain that when you come back, that you've done your best to develop an action plan as to how you're going to improve those areas."

Sometimes it's simple for the employee to correct their performance. Sometimes external factors are impacting resolution. We have single moms who have three or four children, and they're having a problem getting to work on time. They' may bring back an action plan that says, "I'm going to buy another car; as it keeps breaking," or "I'm going to work with my supervisor and see if I can move my shift time a half an hour back, so I can get the kids to school and make it to work," something of that sort. If the employee is having difficulty developing the plan but is willing, the supervisor should be offering suggestions and assisting.

In the previous example, the employee may have to convince the rest of her coworkers to reorganize some of their work so she can come to work a half an hour later. The goal of the supervisor is to help the employee achieve her or his plan and be successful.

Also, employees in the decision-making leave step have additional consequences for a certain period of time, such as lower or delayed merit increases. Written and Decision Making Leave steps are in effect for 12 to 18 months. Additional corrective actions on different performance issues are cumulative and count towards advancing to termination.

We stress to our leadership that recognition of achievement of corrective action plans and on-going communications with employees with performance problems is well worth the time invested.

Health care is facing severe workforce shortages and retention is a key strategy. When an employee who is having performance issues can be "turned around," there are significant returns on the investment. Conversely, if a problem employee is not confronted quickly, the cost to a work unit can be significant in lost productivity, errors, safety and impact on co-workers' morale and productivity. For example, there are estimates of the costs of the turnover of a Registered Nurse position are estimated to range from 1 to many times the base salary. Let's assume an average Nurse salary is $50,000; the cost of replacing this Nurse may range from $50,000 to $100,000. Unfortunately, this cost is often hidden or not recognized. Could you imagine, in a manufacturing or other service business, if a manager reported to their supervisor that they had just lost $50,000 to $100,000?

As noted earlier, at Lee Memorial we focus on retention and the subsequent turnover is a strategic priority. Reducing turnover thus has a significant financial impact. Several years ago, our turnover rate was 18% of our 6,000 employees. Today it's around 8%. Assuming $50,000 as the average cost of turnover, this 10% improvement in turnover represents an additional $24,000,000 to our organization's bottom line. How much the corrective action process represents is not known, but I am confident keeping the right people on the bus or giving them another seat or getting them off the bus has a major impact on turnover.

Gross Misconduct

When it comes to committing gross misconduct in the organization, we have possible actions. In cases of gross misconduct, the employee accused of the action is placed on crisis leave pending completion of an immediate investigation. Usually, the Employee Relations function works with department management to determine whether or not the action warrants immediate termination. If so, the employee is terminated. For example, Susan's a radiology technician, and for some reason she gets upset and verbally or physically abuses a patient. She will no longer work for Lee Memorial and will be reported to the appropriate licensing agency.

Susan will have an opportunity to present her case at a formal grievance procedure. The procedure affords Susan the opportunity to present her case to a committee of her peers and two supervisors not from her area in the organization. The committee will hear the arguments from the employee and her immediate supervisors. The committee will then render a "findings of fact" to determine whether or not the appropriate actions according to the health system's policies were taken against Susan. The committee's recommendation to uphold or overturn the action is made to the Senior Leader over that area of the health system.

Sadly, some good employees do stupid things. The action is very severe but may not warrant immediate termination. It may be a learning opportunity for the offending employee. The challenge is to send a very strong message to the employee that they cannot repeat this offense in the future. This is when a "Final Warning" is invoked. We have a nurse who has a good work and performance record. The nurse decides to access a patient's medical record that she is not authorized to view or gives out unauthorized medical information about a patient to whom she is providing care. It would not be in the best interest of Lee Memorial to lose a valued asset like this nurse over a moment of misjudgment or indiscretion. However, the health system cannot tolerate future offenses like this, as they may have significant consequences. As long the nurse does not repeat this offense, no further corrective action is taken. However, if the offense is repeated, the nurse would be immediately terminated with no right for grievance.

As noted, the grievance process is fairly formal. Being a public health care organization, we believe our level of accountability is even higher than private organizations. Operating in the public in Florida provides many challenges, but I also believe these challenges make our organization even stronger. For example, we have a publicly elected, non-partisan board of directors. Both print and electronic news media attend our board meetings. Ironically, we even have our competitors in attendance at times. Our level of integrity and honesty has to be held at the very highest standard at all levels in our health system.

We want to make certain that our grievance process can withstand any future litigation. At our grievance hearings, our staff attorney facilitates the hearing and we have a court reporter transcribe. Our Legal department believes the hearing process is a wise investment. If and when you do face litigation, whether there's any substance to it or not, the courts look very favorably on having a peer group grievance process prior for terminations. Considering the cost of litigation in attorney fees, fines or potential settlements, the grievance process has proven to be quite cost effective.

Jon C. Cecil is responsible for the overall planning, development, implementation, and operations of a comprehensive Human Resources function for the System. The current employee count for the System is 6,100 employees; it is the second largest employer in Southwest Florida. Recently, Lee Memorial Health was recently recognized and awarded the Employer of Choice by the Herman Group. Lee Memorial joined only 11 other organizations nationally including four other health care organizations that received this award in 2003. In addition, Lee Memorial Health System recently was awarded the 2005 Premier Health Care Employer by J. Walter Thompson, Inc.

He is responsible for strategic planning, operations, policies and procedure related toemployment; human resources information systems; compensation and benefits; labor relations; performance management; workforce planning; employee relations; the human resources service center; and the Flex Staffing Services. He assures compliance with all applicable labor, equal opportunity and other rules and regulations related to the workforce.

Additionally, Mr. Cecil serves as liaison to two Auxiliaries and volunteer organizations with over 3,000 volunteers; has administrative responsibility for the operations of four LMHS Child Development Centers with over 500 children enrolled; and is responsible for the Employee Health and Employee Clinics for the System. Mr. Cecil joined Lee Memorial Hospital in 1972 as a management trainee and held various management and administrative positions. He was promoted to Vice President of Human Resources in 1987. With the affiliation of Sarasota Memorial Hospital and Lee Memorial Health

System in 1997, he accepted the additional position of regional Vice President for Support Services of both health systems. In January 1999, he assumed the responsibility as the System's Chief Human Resources Officer.

The Changing Face of HR

Kathleen T. Geier

Senior Vice President of Human Resources
Goodyear Tire and Rubber Company

The Changing Face of HR

Human capital is one of the most critical areas for developing any company's competitive edge. A company can replicate processes and products, but it is very difficult to replicate people. Therefore, one of my major goals as HR executive is to make sure that the company human resources are is valued as a driver of business success. To do so, I work to develop HR strategies toward a high performance culture, which in part involves making sure that we change with agility as business needs change.

Getting the Right People and Meeting Their Needs

One of the major areas through which HR adds value to this company is in succession planning, because having the right people is critical to making sure the business can meet its goals. Without the right people in place, that just won't happen, so making sure that we have the right people in the right place at the right time can have a tremendous financial impact Identifying them, assessing them, developing leadership, and looking for leadership inside and outside the company is a very important part of human resources.

Compensation and benefit design and rewards and recognition comprise other areas through which human resources has a financial impact. Developing proactive strategies to offset the national crisis of rising health care costs of 11-13 percent annually is a major initiative.

The Ingredients for Success

The art of HR is being able to combine intuitive capabilities with analytical skills. Being able to combine those two elements is essential to successful human resources. Accordingly, the first rule of HR is to listen to the needs of the business. A second rule is to always remember that human capital is an investment and can provide a competitive edge. HR must strive to ensure that the same thought and investment that goes into the purchase and maintenance of expensive equipment should go into the selection and maintenance of people.

An HR executive needs to be a solid business person first and a functional expert second. This perspective is essential in order to be able to understand the business needs and look at human resources from a business viewpoint. He or she also needs consulting skills, the ability to transform organization needs into strategies and plans, a results orientation, market or customer focus, and the ability to clearly create and define human resource metrics.

Part of what human resources executives do is encourage and facilitate change in their companies, so we need to be leaders in change. Our change methodology has focused on a planned change method of helping business leaders develop a business case for the change, then involving key stakeholders in designing the future state "vision" and the action plan to get there. HR used this methodology in 2003-2004 to completely transform HR by using outsourcing as the catalyst for change.

The Win-Win Balance

The biggest challenge of human resources is balancing the needs of the employees with the needs of the business. The best possible outcome is when the needs of both are served in a win-win situation. Although sometimes a choice must be made between the needs of the business and those of the employee, it is ideal to approach such a decision with the goal to find a balance. The decision to outsource one hundred HR positions in 2003 was just such an example. Our business gained cost savings of $45 million over ten years; $21 million in technology cost avoidance and the one hundred positions became new hires for the outsourcing organization. The HR executive must work to retain and motivate associates while making sure the needs of the business are being met. This objective can best be met over time by being clear about communications. Communication must be concise and regular. It must foster a high-performance work environment in which people understand the business and understand the decisions that have to be made. The further away people are from the business, the harder it is for them to understand why some decisions are being made, especially when they are not in their favor. Company leaders need to communicate with their work teams on an interpersonal basis to help them understand the business' goals and how their jobs contribute to achieving them.

HR Within the Organization

It is important that the human resources executive comprehends the positions of everyone with whom he or she works. As head HR executive, I work closely with the chairman, CEO & president, and must therefore understand what he feels is important, not just for human resources, but for the direction of the entire company. We strive to foster a culture that drives high performance, and it is my duty to have a solid grasp on this culture so that I can work to realize it.

Other functional leaders such as the chief financial officer, the chief technology officer and the leader of global communications are my peers, and I do work with them on a regular basis. I try to help the CFO with organization and work with him on compensation and benefit issues. I also spend a good portion of time with the seven business unit leaders of the company, each of whom represent different regions of our company. With these individuals, I must understand what it is that they need to run their business. They each have HR leaders assigned to them, but I also need to work with them because there are both local and global HR points that they need to receive. The more global matters that I provide include a succession planning format, guidelines for rewards and recognition, and guidelines for training and development. Global issues affect the entire enterprise and drives a uniform set of principles and processes. Local or regional processes do the same kind of things but have impact only on that local or regional business team.

The HR Team

HR team members must be change leaders with business acumen. They must be results oriented with a focus on both internal and external customer service. We have a cascading system of goal setting that begins with a corporate document called the OGSM This paper provides a statement of the objective, goals, strategies and measures for the corporation so that in human resources we can determine what we can contribute to that strategy. For example, two of our major strategies are creating and driving a high performance culture and lowering our cost structure. Using that framework, we establish very measurable time or numerically based objectives. We develop an annual operating plan to support the OGSM, and then we do a monthly check to determine whether the objectives are still relevant.

Over the past few years, the role of HR has changed from being a provider of transactional or personnel services to being a business partner. We are now highly involved with developing strategy and determining how the organization will meet its goals, what changes need to be made, and who needs to be brought in. We figure out what competencies the company will require for its success and then decide where we can find talent with those competencies or whether we can develop the people we currently have. We drive the hiring process rather than just doing the paperwork and making sure that they have paychecks and benefits. In the years to come, this role or HR as a strategic business partner will continue to grow. More and more companies will outsource their transactional services, which will allow human resources to focus their energy on more strategic aspects of the business. The benchmarking studies show that a major BPO outsourcing process takes three to five years for all the change metrics to truly rate the success of the change. We are approaching our one-year anniversary and all systems are on target.

Measuring Productivity

Ensuring productivity and growth is an ongoing process that should be monitored on a daily basis. Each person should receive an annual formal evaluation as well as a quarterly review in order to ensure that this progression is occurring. Annually, our people set very measurable objectives and then have periodic meetings to determine how they are or are not working toward them. At the end of the year, they are then appraised on how well they met those goals. On a macro basis, other points can be measured, such as sales and earnings per associate.

Increasing Productivity

Productivity is dependent upon effective prioritizing. It is impossible to get everything done that needs to be done, so supervising managers and HR teams need to be able to decide what should be done in what order. Part of prioritizing is time management and part of it is understanding the business and what is needed. At Goodyear, we go through "blocks of work" exercises in staff organization with which we analyze what needs to be accomplished and what category of urgency it is. If you can visualize the major blocks of work of HR (i.e., recruiting, managing benefits, payroll, etc) and stack them in a pyramid with the strategic block at the top, tactical blocks in the middle, and the transactional (day to day, back office) blocks at the bottom. This process allows you to identify duplication of work – work that can be eliminated or combined or outsourced. We bok at what simply does not need to be done by using the Six Sigma tool to identify waste.

When an employee is non-productive, the first step in addressing the issue is to assess his capabilities and competencies to determine whether anything can be done to improve his efficiency. He may be able to benefit from training or from being put on a special project and then mentored. His deficiency should be addressed so that a development plan may be set. If he fails to progress, then he should be considered for a different role or position for which his skills or competencies may better fit the requirements.

Any improvements that are made should involve employees. Anybody who may be affected by new changes should be a part of the process and in constant communication. If people are involved in determining solutions, they will not feel that they are simply cogs in a machine. They will be more likely to work with the changes.

One technique for increasing productivity is lean management. This is a continuous improvement methodology that involves looking at a whole process and determining where waste can be eliminated. For example, baking a cake requires a series of processes -- but most cakes have a cooking time of an hour. The total time from start to finish of preparing the ingredients to "cooling" the cake after it leaves the oven can be two to three hours. Lean Management would look at every phase of this cooking process to reduce or eliminate "wait time" or preparation time to get us close to the one hour as possible. We do the same for work processes.

Sustaining Productivity

If a company has a base line against which it can measure progress toward improvement, then progress can be monitored. Essential to this progress is involving employees in setting the measures and setting the plan to reach those measures.

Productivity assessment in a production environment can be based on output and associate hour cost per unit. One incentive for increasing productivity is having people share profits that come from increased productivity. Non-monetary incentives such as recognition, performance reviews, letters of commendation, team meeting celebrations for exceeding customer expectations, write-up in company news letters on exceptional performance are effective motivators as well. Sometimes a simple "thank you" can be very meaningful for an employee.

Technology and Productivity

Technologies such as the Internet and e-mail are a dual-edge sword. These tools make communication faster and make working with the world across time zones a possibility. Before electronic communications, interacting with people in China or Europe was incredibly difficult. Enhancing communications enhances productivity. On the other hand, sometimes it is too easy for people to write e-mails rather than see a person face-to-face. Human interaction can occasionally be a more effective exchange than that which occurs over computer screens. It's important to limit the amount and size of e-mails so that it encourages people to see others to get their message across. Rate this face-to-face behavior during annual performance reviews.

Kathleen T. Geier was elected senior vice president of human resources, for The Goodyear Tire & Rubber Company on Aug. 6, 2002. She had been appointed to that position on July 1.

Ms. Geier is responsible for developing and executing a global human resources trategy for Goodyear and ensuring that HR initiatives are in place to drive the company's competitiveness in the marketplace. Prior to her new assignment, Ms. Geier served as director of human resources for Goodyear's Eastern Europe, Africa, Middle East region, based in Brussels.

From 1996 to 1999, she served as director, human resources central services for North America business units and corporate staff in Akron. From 1995 to 1996, she was director, human resources employment practices and HR systems, and director, salaried HR & employment practices from 1994 to 1995, both in Akron.

Ms. Geier's operational experience included assignments as plant manager in Mt. Pleasant, Iowa, from 1992 to 1994, where she managed an industrial and automotive hose manufacturing facility and served as president of Goodyear's Cosmoflex subsidiary in Hannibal, Mo. From 1990 to 1992 she was business center manager for Goodyear in its St. Marys, Ohio engineered products plant and from 1986 to 1990 she was operations manager for Cosmoflex.

After beginning her Goodyear career as a trainee in Akron in 1978, Ms. Geier moved to Gadsden, Ala., as an industrial engineer, followed by Akron assignments in human resources from 1983 to 1986.

The Akron native was born Aug. 7, 1956. She received a bachelor of science of degree in biology and psychology from Heidelberg College in Tiffin, Ohio, in 1978.

Recognizing Team Efforts in HR

Lisa Courtney
Corporate Vice President, Human Resources
Team Health

Recognizing Team Efforts in HR

Human Resources leaders continue to struggle to evolve into a strategic partner with the executives of the company. Many Human Resources executives complain that their executives do not see them as a real strategic player. However, there is a great deal that Human Resources leaders (executives) can do to impact and change the perception their executives and the company has about them and the overall Human Resources team.

Human Resources leaders must understand the business - In order to succeed and be accepted as a Human Resources leader it is important to understand what your company does and why. This information can be obtained by regular communication with your superiors. Evolving into a strategic player means that the Human Resources executive understands the business side of the company. CEO's respect Human Resources leaders who can speak articulately about the business as well as provide insight into potential value that the Human Resources team can add. It is critical to remember that when the company is financially healthy everyone benefits!

Human Resources leaders must align Human Resources with the goals and objectives of the company. I see the goal of the successful leader is to provide Human Resources services aligned with the company's mission and vision. As a healthcare company we are dedicated to advancing exceptional patient care through leadership, innovation and teamwork. While Human Resources may not actually provide patient care, we do work closely with senior management to ensure support of Human Resources initiatives. Without top-down support a Human Resources department loses its strategic influence and ability to impact. Often Human Resources executives underestimate the need to communicate with the top-level executives. The results can be a Human Resources team that is viewed as more administrative and not utilized as a consultative resource able to coach and advise executives. Therefore, frequent communication with the key stakeholders is critical to ensure that priorities and goals meet the needs of the organization.

The Human Resources leader must be able to demonstrate results. The Human Resources team provides many services for the company it is the role of the Human Resources executive to make sure those results (e.g. low turnover, competitive pay and benefits, ability to minimize Human Resources related lawsuits, etc). Without the support of the Human Resources executive, the Human Resources team does not have a sponsor to taut accomplishments—that is a lot like getting up to bat, hitting a homerun and forgetting to run the bases.

The Value of HR

Building a Successful Team

A key contribution that Human Resources makes to the organization is the people who work there. In most cases, Human Resources is involved in recruiting employees as well as providing programs to retain employees. Retention programs include competitive pay strategies, training, benefits, consultative services (being there when employees and managers need a neutral third party), employee relations, etc. Hiring the right people the first time builds a team of competent professionals who can impact the furtherance of company goals and objectives. When someone is hired who is not a good fit, then the entire team is impacted because other team members are having to step in and to the work and employees who are not happy destroy the morale of their co-workers.

Process Improvement

As Human Resources works to become more strategic, benchmarking and metrics are important to the Human Resources Executive. This can be done through a variety of methods. The bottom line is that each core competency within and organization can be benchmarked for best practices. In benchmarking, the employee(s) who obtain the best results are identified and their practices documented. Those practices that drive the best results are incorporated into job descriptions and employees are trained on any changes in procedures for their positions. Our company has found that utilizing work groups to identify best practices is essential. Work groups allow employees to have input and contribute to the overall success of the team.

Also, metrics (or measurements) is important. Our Human Resources group applies metrics to the services we provide our organization. As a result, we can report to managers key information needed to make decisions regarding employee management. Key information includes headcount, current open positions, time to fill positions, cost per hire, benefit cost per participant, turnover statistics, details on why employees leave our company, etc. The goal of sharing this key information is to drive information to the manager to influence reducing turnover and managing costs.

Training and Employee Development

Providing managers and employees with tools necessary to be able to do their jobs and fit into the culture of the organization is essential. Within our organization Human Resources strives to provide employees with orientation programs that allow news hires to be educated on who we are and what we do. Through annual performance feedback and maintenance of current job descriptions, the Human Resources team is able to help employees and managers to communicate with each other regarding performance and career development.

Managing Legal Liability

Human Resources is also a valuable asset in ensuring compliance with state and federal laws. This can be done by subscribing to services (books, websites, newsletters, etc.) that detail the federal and state laws. Additionally, having policies that address legal obligations and training on those policies are important so that both managers and employees understand the company's obligation to state and federal compliance. Many companies have a "hotline" (toll free number) where employees can call to report violations of policy and law. Identifying "hot topics" such as sexual harassment, discrimination, employee coaching, and training managers and employees on these topics helps to avoid potential wrongful acts that could result in lawsuits. The bottom line is that if Human Resources can work to avoid lawsuits, the employees and managers are not distracted by the interrupter of preparing for a lawsuit.

Human Resources is an Art

The art of Human Resources is the ability to practice common sense in understanding how and when to do the right thing while applying specific principles of management, policy and theory. Success in these areas requires the HR practitioner to be flexible in the ability to assess, problem solve and deliver products and services aligned with the organizations objective. The "art of human resources" demonstrates to senior management how to get things done rather than providing ten thousand reasons of why it cannot be done. It is always important to remember there can be more than one right answer and that not every issues is worth going to war over.

Qualities of the Successful HR Executive

Flexibility - A Human Resources executive must be flexible and adaptable, especially when it comes to understanding and meeting the organization's goals and objectives. If the Human Resources executive is dogmatic and rigid, then senior management will work around them instead of work with them. Additionally, the employees will not want to work with Human Resources because of the negative connations that can be derived from a strict and inflexible Human Resources leader.

Visionary - It is critical to see the big picture of the organization and how the people fit into it. Key to the company's mission and vision are the people who make up the team and help to create, maintain and achieve the vision.

Focus on the Right Stuff - It is important that Human Resources leaders not be sidetracked by focusing on minute details such as completing forms, attendance policies, etc. While these may have their place and be important they are concerns that subordinates within the Human Resources team can address. It is easy and tempting to get caught up in the small stuff (e.g. paperwork, policy, etc.) and forget the larger people issues.

Problem Solving Rather than Policing—Human Resources leader who is sensitive to the needs of management and the organizations' employees will be a leader who can identify problems and offer solutions. Human

Resources can get stereotyped as the "police" of the organization. However, a good Human Resources leader will attempt to anticipate problems through applying experience, research knowledge and common sense.

HR and the Healthcare Industry

Human Resources in the healthcare industry faces a unique set of challenges including the shortage of healthcare professionals, the increasing cost of professional liability insurance (malpractice insurance), decreasing reimbursements (Medicare, Medicaid, etc.) and slim profit margins.

Currently there is a significant shortage of nurses, physicians and ancillary support. Fewer students are selecting healthcare as a profession often due to the long hours and low compensation. In addition to attempting to manage costs, managed care has decreased provider (physician, nurse practitioner, nurse anesthetist, physician assistant, etc.) pay. This makes the long years of education and training unappealing.

Another major impact to the healthcare industry is the increasing malpractice lawsuits. While there are some physicians who commit malpractice, there are also frivolous lawsuits. The number of lawsuits, as well as their outcome, drives the costs of malpractice insurance (or professional liability insurance) to unaffordable levels. Many physicians leave their practices because they cannot afford the malpractice coverage.

Another byproduct of managed care is decreasing reimbursements. Healthcare companies and physicians get paid by health insurance companies, Medicare, Medicaid and patients (self-pay). All third-party payers are only paying a percentage of the actual cost of the services provided. The result is the need to run more efficiently and increase patient volumes.

These challenges in healthcare result in companies being able to have fewer HR professionals providing services and the requirement to manage overhead cost in an aggressively lean manner. Having fewer HR professionals can impact quality of service. For example, hiring the right types of employees can be impacted and having time to adequately assess situations before action can result in more errors. These challenges require HR leaders to work as smart as possible and this means only doing work that adds value to the organization. An example of working smarter is an environment where practices are standardized and complex exceptions are eliminated. Each exception to the standard practice results in extra time that could be invested in employee training, manager coaching, etc.

Successful HR Strategies

Listen, Listen, and Communicate

An effective HR person needs to be able to listen and listen. Listening means do not talk and pay close attention to what others are saying. Concise communication cannot occur until we fully understand the needs and expectations of those around us (e.g. management and employees). Listening will make sure that situations are seen from all sides and allow the Human Resources professional to maintain a neutral perspective.

Be Open to New Ideas

While listening and communicating, we need to be open to new ideas and possibilities. It is important to realize that there is often more than one right answer to most problems. One way to be open to new ideas and others is to use empathy as a technique to get into the shoes of the other person, whether that person is an executive or line employee, before making key decisions or communicating important information.

Attitude is Everything

A positive attitude will be contagious to the HR team as well as the entire company including senior management, executive applicants and other employees. An HR team that is motivated and happy will invigorate and inspire others to be happy as well. It is no secret that we often hire people who are just like us, so happy people will attract happy people. HR leaders need to be seeking out ways to recognize and appreciate team members.

Challenges

Resources

A significant HR challenge is being required to do more with less, whether that means less people, less time or less money. I overcome this shortage by establishing and benchmarking best practices, ensuring that what my team members and I are doing really adds value to the organization, driving standardization of best practices to help eliminate costly exceptions, using technology to drive efficiency, and continuing looking at ways to improve processes to eliminate potential waste of time and money. It is very helpful to employ these techniques in order to ensure that we are not being wasteful with any of our resources, especially when those resources are limited.

Expenses

It is also challenging to find means of providing quality benefits at a reasonable cost. The utilization of health insurance benefits is very high and this drives the costs of delivering the service. This rise in cost continues to be hard for employees to understand. To deal with this challenge we have a self-funded health insurance program and we have made changes to drive cost sharing to the highest utilizers.

Providing and managing HR services for 6,500 people in 40+ states is a huge task. I overcome this challenge through a combination of employing locally-deployed professionals (we have HR practitioners at sites having over 250 employees) and implementing a centralized HR staff at the corporate office. These professionals provide both on-site and off-site services utilizing telephones and computers to deliver turn-key HR services.

Working with Other Executives

While I work with all executives within our organization, I work mostly closely with our CEO, President/COO, EVP of Finance (to whom I report) and affiliate Presidents, who are heads of our wholly owned subsidiaries located throughout the US. I have found that understanding our business, meaning the services we provide how we provide them and how we are reimbursed for them, has enabled me to develop a rapport with executives at all levels. Without a working knowledge of what we do for the big picture, I could not be respected nor could I relate to what these people do. Knowing our company first and then being the HR subject matter expert second has paid off in my ability to work as a team with these executives to support key initiatives in our company as well as protect our HR initiatives. While they do work with me to ensure total success, I have found the burden is really mine, as an HR executive, to foster the cooperation and establish the understanding of a need for what my group can do for our organization.

The HR Team

Everyone in Human Resources needs to possess the perspective, flexibility, interpersonal skills and expertise of HR that is required of a good executive in this field. Our team meets regularly just to communicate what is currently going on in our respective areas. In setting goals, I communicate my understanding of senior management expectations and then the team brainstorms on how to best set the goal to meet the need. In both group and individual meetings, follow-up occurs to ensure that goals are met.

The State of HR Today

The biggest change in HR today is continuing to do more with less. We have lost one employee from our head count due to not being able to replace that employee when she resigned. We are very careful in how we spend all resources. It can get frustrating and tiring to continually work to provide expert services in a fast paced, high quality environment with fewer people and fewer resources.

Technology and outsourcing continue to grow in popularity and availability. As HR professionals and company's continue to do more with less, technology makes it possible to provide national HR support and services to a geographically diverse group in real time. Outsourcing forces us to look at why do we exist and does it make sense for us to continue to do certain tasks. Outsourcing non-core tasks can prove to be an effective way to manage time and resources.

Rules to Follow

While there are probably ways to name a million HR rules, I find keeping things simple works best. So I identified three rules of HR that are linked to the necessary skills that I have explained.

The first is to listen carefully. Listening is the foundation of understanding, and understanding is necessary in order to reach viable goals as a department and a company. I think that talking less and listening more will lead an HR executive to success.

An HR person needs to learn constantly. By doing so, we can find flexibility and perspective. Without a desire to learn, it is easy to lose step with the company as well as the HR profession as a whole.

Finally, it is essential to learn how to adapt quickly. Those who cannot adapt will be left behind every time.

The Basics of Employee Loyalty

The foundation to fostering employee loyalty is providing a job with tasks that utilize the skills of the employees in an environment that is supportive and pleasant. It is also valuable to demonstrate a career path so that employees who like their jobs and work environments can feel they have a future within the organization.

A company that feels an absence of loyalty should reevaluate how the jobs are being performed. Are the right people in the right jobs? Do employees need training? Training will help ensure that employees understand how to do their job and feel supported in the ability to do their job, which is essential to the first facet of employee loyalty. If the employees feel the company has invested in them through training, they feel appreciated by their manager and are more loyal.

However, training cannot overcome issues with work environment such as lack of management, recognition or mentoring. A company lacking loyalty needs to evaluate the work environment and make sure that employees are recognized for their efforts.

Benefits and Compensation

Benefits actually play a relatively small role in employee loyalty. Employees may use compensation and benefits as an excuse to leave a company, but in most instances there is a root cause that usually goes back to their manager. However, health, retirement and welfare plans are seen as obligatory by employees. Value adding benefits can also include on-site daycare and health and fitness programs.

If employees are satisfied with their jobs and their manager, compensation is typically not much of an issue. However, if the employee is already dissatisfied, then compensation becomes a bigger issue. In today's younger employee's job satisfaction is hinged on what they do, often how much they make is more secondary.

Reviews

Reviews should accomplish three primary tasks. They should reinforce feedback that has been given throughout the year, review established performance goals for the year and set new goals for the upcoming year. The review should be a time that has been agreed upon in advance for the manager to address these issues. The manager should prepare in advance for the review. Also, it is good for the manager to ask the employee to self-evaluate. A self-evaluation is a good indicator on the communication that has occurred throughout the year.

The review is an opportunity for the manager to reinforce support that has been given throughout the year. It is a formalized mechanism in which the employee receives feedback. This feedback not only includes ways the employee can improve, but should also include recognition for areas where the employee has excelled. If a review is done well, it can leave the employee feeling appreciated and with a sense of purpose. If the review is the only time the employee receives performance feedback, then the review can actually be a tense and adversarial experience.

Loyalty within Departments

In today's fast-paced, geographically diverse world, offsites must work. Offsites work when supported by good technology (e.g. phone systems, computers, etc.) and recognition by all players that offsite relationships require some extra effort because you do not have the in person interaction that often enables camaraderie and rapport.

Common Goals

Often those employees who are making the products or delivering the services will bond around the actual process of understanding what the company does and how it is done. Within my organization, sales and operations have the strongest sense of teamwork for this reason. Often the infrastructure or overhead departments may be more challenging to foster teamwork because they are further removed from the delivery of the product or service. These areas can be Accounting, Finance, Information Technology and Human Resources. Teamwork and loyalty are fostered through managers providing employees with positive feedback including recognition of a job well done. Employees must feel that they have a valuable role within the company otherwise they will not feel loyal. While it is said that business and personal world should remain separate, the manager must make a personal impact on the employee by showing interest in their work and allowing the employee input.

New Strategies for Fostering Loyalty

As more people work remotely, loyalty will depend on the company's ability to educate employees on who the company is and what the company does as well as demonstrating the value and input the employee can add to the company. Companies should focus on how to positively stimulate and manage the employees they have.

The job market can induce loyalty for a period of time, but it is just a temporary fix to a turnover problem. The next twelve months will likely bring more employee shortages and a tight job market due to the retirement of the baby boomer generation.

Lisa Courtney is widely recognized as a leader in the Human Resources profession with over 20 years of experience. While at Team Health, Inc. Mrs. Courtney has played a key role in overseeing the entire Human Resources function of a healthcare staffing company with over 6,000 employees in 43 states and approximately $1.2 billion in revenue. Mrs. Courtney served as the president of the Tennessee Society for Healthcare Human Resources Administrators (TSHHRA) in 2000-2001 and 2003-2004. She also served as the president of the Tennessee Lawson User Group (TLUG) in 2000-2001. She has received a number of awards including the 2004 American Society for Healthcare Human Resources, National Communication Award for published article, "Human Resources: a Common-Sense Discipline", and the International Association of Administrative Professionals "Executive of the Year" in 2004.

HR in the Education Business

Ruth E. Spencer

Director, Human Resources
Oberlin College

Introduction

There are key elements of efficiency in operations in any organization: having an adequately trained staff, working harmoniously and collaboratively with one other, and in totality having the whole system work better than any single individual part. In a college setting, the need for collaboration is greater than it may be in a company setting because so many departments rely on HR to keep them informed on how the system works and the different dynamics within it.

Considering the long-term consequences of solutions is a significant element of a college's HR, because too often people are looking for quick fixes. Quick fixes generally do not solve a problem in the long run. It is important to understand that the institution is a system in which all of the elements must be addressed. For example in looking at a problem one must look at the people component, the programmatic element and the integration of the project within the greater system to see if it is consistent with the long term goals of the organization. If a wellness program is to be developed how does that impact food service workers vs. faculty in terms of scheduling availability. Does the program meet the needs of a variety of populations on the campus? Does the program meet a long-term goal such as taking a more active role in having a healthy lifestyle.

Directing human resources is much like conducting an orchestra. It is composed of many different parts that must work together harmoniously so that the system can truly perform. If there is discord in one section of an orchestra, it will affect the entire group. Similarly, if one worker is disgruntled or inefficient, the whole department may become dysfunctional.

To prevent situations like this, HR should check to see if upcoming changes will be supported by all other systems that may be affected. If HR decides to make a change of a code number within an integrated HRIS system what other systems will be impacted? Will benefits or payroll be impacted or just the personnel data registry?

Success in Human Resources

Successful HR executives must truly like people. They have to enjoy listening to, working with, and making decisions for and with other people. Too often the people part of human resources is eclipsed by the desire to get something done, but the fact is that no matter how good the technology or system, the job will not get done if people are unhappy. It is important that HR offers a sense of fairness and equality so that people feel they have a place to turn.

I advise my staff to never react too quickly. It is important to think through the problem before coming up with a solution. Jumping into an issue before thoroughly considering it rarely yields positive outcomes.

When a problem arises, it is important to listen to the people posing the problem. HR executives should not necessarily insist on people making appointments all the time either. In certain situations, waiting for an appointment only delays peoples' sense of response and makes them more upset. I always try to assess the person who is coming to me and why he or she wants to speak with me. Then I decide whether it is better to see him or her immediately or whether the matter can wait for an appointment.

The HR Team

HR people must be able to work collaboratively while being able to ask challenging questions. It is critical not to only have "yes people" on the team because they tend to not critically assess situations in order to develop better solutions. I believe it is best for my team members to be better at what they do than what I do. If they are stronger at their part of the system and can collaborate for the greater good, then we will be able to make a positive impact. That sense of team and work ethic is extremely important. Find a way to commit to what is important to individuals as well as what is important to the department. Individuals want to be valued and not feel like they are widgets. There has to be a good balance between meeting the needs of staff and the greater good of the organization.

As the director of HR at a college, I work closely with the division heads. It is central to the role of HR that we understand not just the rules, but also the needs of the people with whom we work. Whether we are asked for advice on dealing with advertising or a poorly performing employee, we need to be capable of assessing the situation, the needs of the people, the needs of the institution, and how we can best communicate a solution.

Setting Goals as Individuals and as a Team

To establish objectives, I ask the team what projects we should undertake collaboratively. I then ask each person to set his or her own personal goal for the project For example, we may decide to implement three upgrades in our HRIS system. We then determine what we need to do that and what training will be necessary. Then each person will identify something that they can contribute to that project and each person will identify something that they want to do for themselves in their own learning process. Due to our process, our staff is quick to identify and suggest more creative and comprehensive solutions rather than always waiting for me to dictate what will be done.

Changes in Human Resources

The information piece of HR has changed significantly in the past few years. The technology with which we collect information has advanced and threatens to run faster than the people who use it. HRIS systems have become very sophisticated, so we need to strive to stay on top of the technology. If only one person in the office can access information, then the system will only hold us hostage if that person leaves. Technology will continue to challenge us and we must work to use it efficiently and effectively. We need to be able to put the information in more quickly so we can rapidly receive the data in more comprehensive formats. Oberlin is in the process of creating on line testing or new applicants and those seeking promotions in the technical and clerical positions. Our IT people review any and all project specifications and provide maintenance to existing programs. They are critical partners in any technical undertakings.

Our connections with insurance carriers and the information that they give us have also changed. We use this information to identify trends for general disease management programs for employees, utilization of hospitals and specialized medical services. We believe that education regarding preventative care will impact our health care costs by 5 to 10 percent over the next five years.

The regulations set forth by HIPPA (Health Insurance Portability and Accountability Act) have affected HR as well. HIPPA has influenced how and to whom we give information regarding medical illness. We look much more carefully as to who has a need to know the details of why a n employee is absent for medical leave. We now have a dedicated fax that goes only to the benefits coordinator for medical release forms to improve confidentiality.

HR Basics

Above all, HR people must remember to always be honest. People in human resources are often viewed as nay sayers because we are the ones who have to tell people in the organization what they can and cannot do regarding employment decisions such as hiring, firing, promotions, etc. For that reason, it is important for us to have reasonable and true explanations as to why we have to say no.

Accordingly, it is essential to not do anything that cannot be defended with a rational reason. It is not an adequate response to simply say that something is being done because it is the rule. HR people must be able to communicate why the rule exists.

Policies and procedures don't work without people. People are the reason why policies and procedures are in place and they decide whether or not they will be respected. Persons who decide not to follow rules often don't feel the rules have taken into consideration their circumstance. They behave with the mindset of how can I avoid the rule or policy or they may say it is not important that this rule or policy be adhered to. For example, I found this candidate that I like and I will hire them even if they don't meet the requirements that I have published in the job posting, ignoring that there are qualified applicants that have been rejected. Persons have to understand why making such decisions will have adverse consequences to the institution or company.

Backing-up Diversity

Workforce diversity has come very far in the sense that most people can now understand why it is important. The problem we face, however, is actually making diversity a reality. Organizations must take care to actually give people equal opportunities rather than just saying that they will. They must look at their own biases in terms of the process and consider how and what they communicate. There should not be a disconnect between a diversity policy and how it is applied. A good diversity policy is one that is realistic, attainable and transparent to the total workforce community.

Obtaining feedback from employees can serve a large role in ensuring that workplace diversity is not just empty talk. Interviewing employees, both minorities and non-minorities, at intervals of employment can provide valuable information as to the supportiveness of the workplace to fostering a welcoming atmosphere for all people. This gives employers feedback about the impact of their efforts to make all people feel welcome and supported. Interviewing persons who have left often provides insight on the real feelings of individuals. Oftentimes these individuals may not have been eager to provide that information while they were at the institution.

An institution can specifically strive and take steps to be more diverse and multicultural. To actively pursue diversity, an institution needs to do more than the norm. They need to advertise exceptionally. For example, we target minority Ph.D. candidates from many different programs and send them information about our institution. In terms of higher education, it can be helpful to advertise to historically black colleges and network with mentor programs. It is not enough to simply put an advertisement in the paper.

Ensuring Fair Salaries

We have made a good deal of progress in the area of ensuring that salaries are fairer and that different people get paid equal amounts for the same job. It is good to look at what salaries are exactly. The continuing salary needs to be considered as well as the starting pay, because the starting salary is often not where the big discrepancies occur. If incongruities exist, they need to be explainable. We need to continue to monitor salaries throughout employees' careers, because if discrepancies exist they may not be noticed. We also need to consider the ratios of promotions and professorships for diverse populations within the institution.

The Backlash Against Diversity

The concept of white males not getting a fair shake has become a rallying cry in some places where reverse discrimination claims are cropping up.

This backlash has and does set us back. These claims tie up both financial and human resources. We must confront these cases with facts and identify that these claims are being brought by persons who feel threatened that their power and opportunity has been diminished when factually it has not.

Challenges for Minorities

Working mothers seem to have a problem getting part-time employment at any kind of reasonable wage. Flexible and part-time jobs are being created less frequently, which is an issue that needs to be addressed. At Oberlin we have a particularly beneficial program in which mothers can take two months leave and then enjoy job security for the rest of the year if they need to stay out. This is a fairly unique program, so often there is a big consequence for mothers taking time off. The result is Balancing the cost of child care versus the wages earned is a real problem for many families. The consequence of being out of the workforce impacts income and career advancement for women.

Minorities continue to face challenges in being evaluated fairly. All too frequently individuals are seen as not being able to do their job if confronted with certain kinds of problems. For example, a president may believe that one minority may have difficulty terminating another if put in that position. Administrators who have doubts should be honest and ask. All too often they act on their own assumptions and fears which is when prejudices become acts of racism and discrimination.

Developing a Workforce Diversity Policy

When a college or company addresses the problem of workforce diversity, the inclusion of long-term planning is critically important. They need to evaluate how they want their workplace to look and how they can plan it to look like that. And if they do not have minorities at the table for decision making, then it is a farce.

The starting point to developing a policy is recognizing the need for a diverse workforce. Once the goal is set, a plan to achieve it can be made. The institution needs to identify a desire on a systemic level and then speak to people from different backgrounds who are current employees. Those people need to be asked why they stay with the institution and what could make their workplace a more welcoming setting. Then any minorities who have left the organization need to be asked why they chose not to stay. Such information will allow the institution to make real change and not simply provide lip service to change.

e-Learning

Keeping Informed About New Programs

People in charge of e-learning can stay on top of new programs by visiting other entities that use e-learning. It is critically important to see other models and examples in order to recognize how fast this technology is changing and how improvements can be made. One should look at who are the users? How versatile is the program for different groups of employees? What kind of feedback have the users given? Are those who purchased the program getting what they thought they were buying?

The Impact of e-Learning

E-learning programs can keep current the skills of employees because they are so quickly and readily updated. They are effective in teaching employees new programs so that, for example, a secretary can learn Excel at an advanced level very quickly. Instead of spending years learning a more complex system, an employee can learn it within months. As departments gain new information, people can be trained on it quickly. However, employers need to understand that all employees do not learn the same way. Some people learn better in the group process.

These programs are rather expensive right now, running between $30,000 and $50,000. Cost benefit analysis should be done on such programs. The prices hopefully will come down as more businesses provide such services.

The savings offered through e-learning need to be demonstrated in how much shorter they make the learning curve. Once people learn new programs, information can be gathered to measure their results. Pretest and post-test results can be evaluated. The time involved and the complexity of the function are a part of that evaluation. It is important to have people partner in the development of new programs so that someone can be onsite intermittently to address what is being learned and how it can be applied.

If people aren't using the programs regularly, however, they become just another book on the shelf. Training cycles can help engage employees, as can regularly scheduled e-learning activities.

Trends in e-Learning

E-learning can be used to administer standardized tests during the hiring process in order to ensure that people actually possess the skills that they claim to have. The quality of new hires will improve because the learning curve will be much shorter on the technical side. The people interaction side will still have to be addressed. E-learning will communicate the need for technical competence at entry level. The down side to this is that there will be fewer jobs where every task is on the job learning.

Ruth E. Spencer has been the Director of Human Resources at Oberlin College in Oberlin, Ohio since 1995. She brings education and applied practice in both psychiatric social work and law to her profession. Although her primary expertise is in labor relations, employment law and employee relations, the values of professional social work transcends all of her individual and systemic decisions. Ms. Spencer has been involved in her communities on both local and national levels. She has been a board member of the Women's Funding Network and Lambda Legal Defense Fund. She is currently is the board president for Hitchcock Center for Women in Cleveland, Ohio. Ms. Spencer is also an adjunct assistant professor at the Smith College School for Social Work in their graduate clinical program. She has over ten years of experience teaching in both undergraduate and graduate higher education. Ms. Spencer has participated on numerous panel discussions and presented in both local and national venues. Ms. Spencer is the recipient of the "Changing the Face of Philanthropy "award from the Women's Funding Network, the "Oberlin College Distinguished African American Alumni Award" and for 2002 and 2003 was a Bertha Capon Reynolds Fellow at the Smith College School for Social Work. Ms. Spencer embodies 30 years in social work, 22 years in law, 20 years in human resources administration, and 10 years of higher educational instruction.

Dedication: *I would like to acknowledge the wonderful and competent Human Resources staff at Oberlin College with whom I have had the pleasure of learning and laboring with for the past nine years.*

The World of HR: Communication, Culture, and Compensation

Robert G. Hennemuth

Vice President, Human Resources
Jacuzzi Brands, Inc.

HR: The Role and the Impact

The role of HR is to enable business success through strategies and partnership and to help improve the effectiveness of the people charged with achieving the business' goals and objectives. Once a merely transactional function, today's HR team is comprised of strategists who think of themselves first as business people, and second as HR leaders. At Jacuzzi Brands, our HR team focuses on three important areas to help our company achieve its goals: organizational capability, communication and culture, and executive leadership and compensation.

Organizational capability is the first of three areas on which I focus as the vice president of human resources. I strive to continuously improve the capability of this organization at all levels. We focus on campus recruiting to bring fresh ideas and tomorrow's leaders into the company. This is not an "HR exercise." I recall one MBA recruit who after a month on the job, developed a software solution that significantly improved line fill at our largest customer **and** reduced our inventory by $1M. We also create focused developmental actions to strengthen our middle management and ready them for executive opportunities, and we review the organizational structure on an ongoing basis to ensure that it stays in constant alignment with the changing priorities of the business.

The second area is communication and culture. Having a clearly defined culture is critical to any business, but within that culture it is important to maintain a series of communication platforms that leaders can rely on to reinforce that culture. In today's global workplace, clear communications and a shared company culture are the critical enablers to leveraging the collective contributions of people who come from different geographies and cultural perspectives.

Our third focus is on executive leadership and compensation. Leadership succession and compensation actions require considerable planning and benchmarking in today's environment of intense public and regulatory scrutiny. It is incumbent on the senior human resource executive to facilitate these issues working closely with the Compensation Committee of the Board of Directors, their outside compensation advisors, and executive management.

Of my responsibilities within those areas, the one with the greatest business impact is finding the right leaders. Selection is actually more important than development because if the wrong individual is chosen for a position, it is very difficult to remedy through development actions. I work to develop the right skills and processes to make the right pick. Executive recruitment requires a sound assessment methodology to calibrate a candidate's motivation, skills, personality, and ability to handle complexity. In-depth reference checks are essential—I always do my own—and the executive's stylistic "fit" with the culture needs careful consideration. More than once I have supported the hire of a talented executive with great qualifications and references only to see the person struggle to fit with the people and culture. For this reason, we work hard to create an atmosphere that welcomes stylistic differences, but at the same time we seek confirmation about an executive's style from references.

Organizations frequently must change their structures, so it is important to educate people on the necessity of a business that can adapt to new developments. I work with line executives to structure the organization so that it can keep pace with change and that has a definite financial impact. Since organizational structures always set parameters and focus people in certain directions, people will often focus on achieving an objective that has been overcome by events in the marketplace, unless the structure stays adaptive. We work hard with our line managers to help them see structure as a tool to address an issue, rather than a reflection of their personal status. My COO always speaks of building "temporary bridges" rather than elaborate structures that are harder to change. We would rather get across the divide quickly and keep moving, than take a longer time to build a more permanent solution to a fluid situation.

A more concrete manner in which I create financial value for my organization is managing the cost of benefits. This expense has an enormous inflationary negative attached to it, so it is essential to constantly redesign them in order to manage their costs. We work hard to leverage more value out of our benefits plans by helping employees understand what they have, and designing the benefits to address the most important priorities of our employees. We want our employees to view their benefits in the context of their total compensation so they can appreciate the trade-offs we choose to make.

Finding Success in HR

The HR executive needs to know the business and know the people. It is his duty to measure the gap between the people and the critical business objectives so that it can be overcome. Every year, a very rigorous assessment process should be pursued through which people at all levels are asked to "size" their human resources relative to their challenges. With a candid and accurate examination, the gap between people and business can be identified and addressed. If the human resource executive possesses a strong business acumen, executive assessment skills, courage, and a breadth of vision, he should be able to partner with his business leader to successfully take the steps necessary to align the people with the organizational goals.

The most effective HR executives have a teachable point of view and a perspective that informs all of the advice that they give to line management. They also have strong communication and coaching skills, since their organization will not be able to benefit from ideas ineffectively conveyed or applied.

Strategies

I believe it is important to take the time at the beginning of every cycle to set very clear HR strategies that are aligned with the business objectives. In order to do this, HR needs to participate in development of both the strategic plan and the annual budget, and then build strategies that align with and supplement those plans. The overarching questions are: Is there alignment between the business objectives and what people are working on? Do we have a pipeline of motivated people with the right skills to meet the business objectives? Are they empowered by leaders and the organizational structure to change tactics and plans as needed? Flexibility is key, because nothing ever happens exactly the way it is expected, and the goal is to get the results we have targeted.

One of the challenging aspects of being in human resources is defining the roles we play. People in organizations hold many different views about what HR people are supposed to do, so we must be very clear with the organization on what we do and don't focus on and why. It is necessary for

HR to prioritize when creating strategies and addressing issues, and those priorities should be based on the business goals. On any given day, a voluminous number of small issues can cross the desk of an HR person. Sometimes they are emotional matters, sometimes they are procedural, and sometimes they are simply not our responsibility. For example, it is not an HR responsibility to discipline a manager's subordinates – that is a core accountability of a leader. Yet I have had dozens of managers over the years send their subordinates "down to see HR."

The Role of HR within the Organization

The senior HR executive must have a good feel for what each of the functions in the company do. He works closely with the CEO, COO, and CFO, as well as the chairman of the compensation committee. The CEO makes business decisions and assessments based on a broader vision of the organization than most other executives do. The role of each corporate officer has changed as a result of Sarbanes-Oxley and the regulatory framework that informs the work of the Board of Directors. As a result, CEO's and the other corporate officers need to be highly attuned to the public nature of executive compensation, succession planning and public relations activities. One of the CHRO's key responsibilities is being externally aware and up to date, in order to help each corporate officer navigate these new waters.

The HR executive also must assemble an effective team. I look for judgment, ambition, adaptability, and thoroughness in my people. Small errors can have a great impact, so conscientiousness is a critical quality, especially in the area of executive compensation. Creativity is also important, but above all, HR people must possess business acumen. They must be able to articulate how the business is doing and stay on top of current business trends. The market moves so fast today that companies need to be in a constant state of adjustment. Since HR is a funnel for communications and the internal dynamics of a company, staying ahead of the power curve is essential. In our company, this priority is captured in one of our corporate values – Sense of Urgency. We constantly challenge ourselves to view time as a resource we seize to our advantage.

Setting Goals

At the start of each year, I hold a session in which I set strategy, provide external learning, and define and assign projects. Each project has clear deliverables and an action plan with a team leader. Depending on the project, I establish periodic reviews to assess progress and identify obstacles quickly. Each member of the HR function has annual measurable objectives based on our chosen strategies.

Changes in HR

In larger companies, the approach to human resources has been greatly affected by companies' increased reliance on technology and outsourcing. Smaller and mid-sized companies are often caught in the middle, with insufficient infrastructure or resources to justify tremendous changes in technology or outsourcing. Still, we look at each administrative task as a potential candidate for outsourcing, and work with our vendors to streamline processes and costs. My HR team sees inefficient or poor administrative processes as the biggest hurdle to delivering the higher value work of coaching, leadership development and talent pool management.

More and more we are expected to influence the business and serve as stewards of our organizations' cultures. This demand is not a new concept, but it is certainly becoming increasingly popular. The number of HR people within organizations may be smaller than in past years, but this trend towards focusing HR people more on strategy and organizational capability and less on administration issues will redefine their roles, and have a more significant business impact.

Rules to Remember

It is essential that a HR executive always keep the interests of the shareholders in mind. HR practitioners balance the interests of many constituencies: the board of directors, managers and executives, the employees and employment candidates. We strive to create a positive and attractive workplace, to retain and develop our human resources, and recruit the best people. As we consider where and how to invest our resources and budgets, I always ask my team one question: This project we are contemplating is really appealing, but is it the right thing to do for the business?

The HR executive must also know what he doesn't know so that he can strive to learn new skills. Learning agility is a key discriminator in executives. The moment an executive loses the desire to learn, it's over. This applies with equal force to the HR executive. The most agile learners thirst for new knowledge and get excited by the unknown.

Finally, the HR executive must always keep his promises. When line executives make cutting remarks about HR, it's usually because we haven't demonstrated that we deliver what we promise. To plan, execute, and deliver must be the price of admission in HR.

Ensuring Fit

Hiring for the future rather than the present is a difficult but necessary strategy when it comes to recruitment. Even if there is a pressing business need and a capable external candidate available to fill it, if that individual will not be able to grow within the organization to fill other needs, then he should rarely be given the position. Every time an organization fills a position with an individual who is "topped out," it creates more risk in the overall objective of matching the talent pool to the future business needs. This is not to say, however, that every hire should be a potential CEO. Every organization functions primarily on the good work of the people in the middle of the bell curve. Ideally, companies should look for a diverse mix of talent, but insist on people with the desire and potential to learn and grow.

In order to prevent poor fits, it is important to maintain very clear and high standards and perform exhaustive reference checks. The candidate's demonstrated effectiveness should be examined so that his or her ambition and experience base can be understood. A candidate should be able to handle the complexity required of the role and possess a balanced, mature character.

Raising the Bar

Hiring the right people has grown more difficult because jobs have become more complex, but the available talent has not necessarily received the right opportunity to develop. It used to be that if a candidate had a good experience base, that would be a solid indication that he or she could work well for another company within that functional realm of experience. However, the jobs that are needed now demand people who are more capable of dealing with business and diverse cultures on a global basis. They have to move three times as fast as they did even last year because cycle times have been reduced. There are not many people who can demonstrate they meet these needs for speed and global perspective, so there is a widening split between what needs to be done and the resources available to accomplish it. In our business, we look for leaders who are extremely comfortable with technology, travel globally, and work with people unlike themselves. For example, we insist executives at all levels communicate by e-mail. Last summer we took our top twenty-five executives to China for a week to explore that market opportunity and shake ourselves lose from our U.S./Europe focus. As a result, we are already reaping the rewards of a more global mindset and orientation.

The Impact of Economic and Political Factors

Since 9/11, the major change in the talent marketplace has been a resistance to relocation. As a reaction to that resistance, many companies are setting the dangerous precedent of allowing executives to leave their families in one state and live for a long period of time in another part of the country or world. This is an acceptable strategy for a period of time, but over the long haul, when a family doesn't move with a new hire, the employee has greater personal stress which can detract from performance. There may also be less of a commitment on his or her behalf to stay in the new location and position, and a view by subordinates that he or she is just "passing through."

Red Flags

I always tell new executives that people have ninety days to establish an image that the organization will have for them for the remainder of their career there. First impressions are important and resilient. If, in those first three months, an executive demonstrates an overly-political orientation, he/she may be "branded" as untrustworthy. If he/she goes into a company and tries to achieve personal stature instead of working towards solid goals, he/she is likely to encounter problems.

Excessive struggles due to character issues or team dynamics can also constitute warning signs. Teams work differently in different companies, yet in every company, once a team dynamic or protocol is established, anyone who fails to recognize and follow that protocol can falter quickly. In a related issue, occasionally a new executive will join an organization with the attitude that he or she will be the "savior" hired to solve all the problems created by predecessors. That attitude creates a red flag, because solutions are never as easy as they may appear.

If it becomes rapidly apparent that a new hire was not a right decision, a careful assessment has to be made. While blatant mis-hires need to be confronted quickly, the odds are often stacked against a new hire, so organizations should not be too quick to jump to conclusions. Companies too often bring their own biases to bear regarding a new hire's style rather than considering with a fresh perspective what that person might bring to the organization over time. Especially at higher levels, new hires need to be shepherded and protected a bit as they integrate into the organization. If a company gains a reputation of being too difficult to break into, that merely reinforces negative aspects of the culture and makes recruitment more challenging.

The Interview Process

If the CFO wants someone who is very technical, the line manager wants someone who is a change agent and the HR person wants someone who will not be as abusive as the prior manager, then they might all focus on different candidates. They have to come to an agreement in the beginning as to the entire candidate profile they want. Otherwise, the process will be slowed down by focusing on people who don't fit the full profile.

I believe that interview questions should be very open ended. Asking people what led them to make a decision elicits far different information than asking what the actual decision was. I frequently ask people what adjectives their peers would use to describe them. I also ask what the most common misconception others may have of them. These questions get at the behavioral side of people and how they view themselves. I seek to discover what kind of learning ability they have and how they are able to respond to feedback.

Background Checks

We check references extensively and perform background checks for most positions. Many companies are moving toward personality assessments, whether standardized or individualized. These tests can be beneficial if a company is willing to make the investment, because they are able to develop relationships with outside industrial psychologists who become familiar with the company. They get to know the players in the company and can have a very candid conversation with the candidate about what they may foresee as potential issues with his or her employment there.

Leadership with Heart

Leadership is not about inspiration. It's about setting context and clear accountabilities. It is about having some measure of fairness and strong assessment skills. It requires being a good coach and bringing energy to the organization. If a leader does these things and possesses these qualities, people will become inspired, but there is no such thing as inspirational leadership.

Training

A critical part of training is establishing a structure of accountability and ensuring that people clearly understand what is expected of them. Training can be expensive and time-consuming, so it is really important to match development actions to a person's career potential *and* the company's needs. Larger organizations often use the top training position as a rotational assignment for line executives, which I think is a terrific way to focus training on what's important to the business.

There is a trend in managers engaging in e-learning activities and reading business books in an effort to improve their management skills. However, there are pivotal moments in an executive's career where formalized course work and mentoring can elevate the individual's perspective and leadership skills. Leadership is neither an art, nor simple to grasp, so the investment in a week-long, intensive leadership course or focused skill development course can pay great dividends for the organization. In every company I have worked for, we have utilized external leadership courses such as those offered by The Levinson Institute or Center for Creative Leadership to help rising executives achieve step-level improvements in their leadership capability.

Connecting with Employees

It is possible to get to know your employees while still preserving the manager/employee relationship. One often sees managers who do not understand their employees. This arises when the manager focuses only on tasks, assignments, and progress without listening or, more accurately, without listening completely.

As an executive, you must constantly ask of yourself one thing, and that is to focus on the moment. When meeting with employees, you need give that moment 100 percent of your attention. If you do so, you will pick up on the subtle cues that you need to understand how your employees are feeling and the issues relevant to the task that you are trying to accomplish.

Non-Financial Motivation

It may be surprising, but financial compensation is rarely the highest motivator in any organization. Other than in the sales function, which attracts people more inclined to measure their success in dollars, monetary compensation has more to do with a sense of fairness. Most employees want three things: rewarding work, recognition, and a good, or fair, wage.

Think back to when you were happiest at work, and I am willing to bet that you recall first how significant or important the project was that you were a part of. People are motivated by work that they find rewarding. Second, we all appreciate recognition for a job well done. There are countless ways to recognize people both individually and in a group setting, and these are very powerful motivational tools.

Changing Management Styles

Some people say that there are trends towards managing with heart. However, I would say that this has to do more with a shift in demographics. The geographic dispersion of the nuclear family, the onset of two-income families, and the fact that employees rarely join a company today expecting to stay there for their career, have changed the applicant pool. Incoming employees want employers to provide them the flexibility now needed in their lives. The workplace has adjusted as a pragmatic response to these different needs. Organizations and employers have a hard time finding the right people with the right skills and experience to get the job done. So, for example, they bend over backwards to create flexible work schedules to appeal to a certain employee base. Furthermore, a lot of companies are letting employees live and work remotely. These actions are pragmatic adjustments, not new leadership theories.

Understanding Diversity

There is also an awakening to understanding diversity, and not only along the lines of sex or race. In the past decade, customers, competitors, and suppliers have all become global. In a global business, diversity is about culture, language, ethnic rivalries, travel, security, and so much more. People value, think, and interrelate in truly diverse ways. Today, organizations need to focus not just on how the employee population looks, but on how they process information, communicate, and grasp cultural differences. In order to attract and leverage the best talent, managers must guard against hiring only people in their own image. An employment candidate with the greatest potential to deliver solutions or results for your business won't accept your offer if she senses that your culture will not accept or appreciate her professional or personal perspectives and style.

Recognition in the Organization

In general, either company-wide or business-unit-wide, having recognition awards is an excellent type of incentive program. These types of awards usually have a financial component, but it is not substantial. More important is its meaning for the individual in the attendant fanfare and excitement. Employees can be nominated for awards in many different categories; quality, company values, energy, or any particular area leaders feel is key to the organization's success. If you communicate to your employees a lot about the award program, when the winners are announced they become role models. That can really go a long way.

In my organization we have just finished a round of nominations for recognition awards which carry a stock award for the recipient. We will be recognizing five people across our company: one for each of our values: performance, sense of urgency, people, innovation, and customer relationships. The winners will be true exemplars of those values. Within the company we will publicly announce the recipients and the reasons for their selection. These five people will join the senior leadership at our next senior leadership meeting for a special recognition dinner. When they go back into the workplace they will spread the word about what the senior leadership believes is truly important.

Healthy Employee-Manager Relationships

In every organization, there are strong leaders and weak leaders. It is critical to take time to teach and give leaders feedback about their performance as leaders. Leaders must be aligned with the organization and responsible for engaging their employees. The good news is that leadership is not charisma or some other natural trait. Organizations that insist on high expectations for their leaders, and take the time to equip them with strong leadership skills, will find themselves with leaders focused on winning. And winning is the elixir of engaged employees.

Robert Hennemuth is Vice President, Human Resources of Jacuzzi Brands, Inc. Mr. Hennemuth joined Jacuzzi Brands from Honeywell International, formerly known as AlliedSignal Inc., where he served as Vice President of Human Resources &

Communications for various businesses, including Honeywell Consumer Products Group. Previously, Mr. Hennemuth was a corporate director of human resources at Raytheon Company. While in that position, Mr. Hennemuth was responsible for labor strategies, management development, training, diversity and staffing.

There are so many fine line executives who have taught me about great leadership. In particular, I am indebted to Don Devine of Jacuzzi Brands, who is a remarkable leader and teacher, as well as Ron Slahetka at Perkin Elmer, Dave Berges at Hexcel Corporation, Dave Lundstedt at Honeywell Consumer Products and Fred Poses at American Standard. I would also thank Lee Burke for her countless insights on leadership, Kaye Veazey of VZ Communications, and Gerry Kraines of The Levinson Institute whose frameworks for executive assessment and leadership run throughout this chapter.

Changing the World of Work

Nancy Hanna

Senior Vice President of Human Resources
Ceridian Human Resource Solutions

Changing the World of Work

Through a series of acquisitions, my company has experienced a great deal of growth and change. This rapid transformation, combined with a dynamic marketplace, created a corporate environment that held challenges for employees at every level, in locations around the world. My role as human resource executive involves pulling together a more connected cultural framework out of what we've become. This objective requires the development of a broad, overarching strategy that incorporates leadership development philosophies and people engagement.

Beyond this general goal, I devote substantial effort to our business, managed human resource solutions. It's an exciting time to be in the HR field, and working at Ceridian presents a very real opportunity to create a model of best practices in human resource management. Part of this element is technical, using our own products, being able to provide input to our product management and product development groups, and being a showcase for potential customers. The other part of this opportunity is the manner in which we are so intrinsically connected to the business. This connection offers us a unique platform for discussion of our own people and our own issues as an organization.

Finally, I work to create a stronger connection between the different global pieces of our business. They had been running fairly independently in the past, and we are finding ways to shift our thinking to be less U.S.-centric and more global, to capitalize on trans-national business opportunities.

Adding Value

The role I perform that has the most financial impact for my company is to get the right people in the right roles at the right time. Talent acquisition in today's environment is a key competitive advantage, and has much more to it than simply finding skills alone. "Fit" is just as important—or even more important. The goal is to find just the right fit without eliminating the creativity of diverse backgrounds, ideas and perspective.

I further add value by influencing employee satisfaction and engagement. Success in this area results in employee productivity, which in turn results in huge gains. Employee engagement entails alignment of individual effort with corporate goals. It's a sure way to add a real focus to all of the efforts across the organization and to make sure we aren't wasting any energy.

Human resources is about balance between business needs and people's motivations. Providing that balance is another way HR adds value; this initiative involves the delivery of fact-based decisions that consider the awareness of human impact. There is a pendulum swing in HR; the pendulum swings between employee advocacy and the business partner. At different points over time, organizations swing one way or the other. Historically, one could argue that HR organizations leaned more towards employee advocacy. Then we saw a push towards business partnership as we asked, "What will it take for HR to get a place at the table?"

Now we are at the table, and human resources is committed to maintaining the right balance. HR is dedicated to being bi-focal at all times. We stay deeply tuned to the distinct balance at our organization, vigorously analyzing what is right for the business, making sure that we are aligned with leadership-desired outcomes. At the same time, we cannot sacrifice the positive elements of our strong role as employee advocate. HR grows stronger when we ensure appropriate communication and connection with the promise and potential that our human resources hold. We flourish when we have an awareness of fairness, when we treat people with dignity and listen to them – no matter where they fall in the organizational chart.

The Qualities for Success

Success for the HR executive demands business savvy and the ability to look at the organization objectively. Success demands that we create the right balance between people and the business. HR executives balance competing forces and dynamics. We find ways to instill in others the kind of creativity and confidence that leads to success. In the future, the organizations that succeed will be those that create and nourish the kind of corporate culture that supports their goals to the fullest. To accomplish this requires a human resources executive whose corporate balance is unerring and whose analytical skills are formidable.

We must also have "systems sight" with which we can look across a whole system and see what's happening at various levels. The best HR effort is both broad and deep. Decentralized corporate structures and disparate processes have created an information disconnect that robs management of reliable information, and operational decisions become less consistent. The corporate environment can feel cluttered and chaotic. As organizations strive to create a corporate structure that is more supple and adaptable, effective HR leadership creates real value by cutting across functional areas and effecting the organization at a uniquely personal level.

Because message is key, HR's comprehensive view of the system has great influence, helping senior executives communicate core values. Working broadly across the organization and deeply within it, HR can drive real value by clearly articulating the benefits of employee engagement and the methods to increase it. Operating in this manner, HR helps institutionalize the very best processes and structures – and that makes the company stronger.

The sharing of knowledge is another way HR's "systems sight" can impact corporate success. Strategic knowledge management is a worthy goal, and the marketplace has seen growing acceptance of formalized business intelligence systems. But I have found that the most effective knowledge management initiative is often one that is much more personal, much more informal, and much more granular in nature.

HR's broad and deep "systems sight" takes on additional importance in discussions of compliance and risk management. In a very real way, individuals are policymakers. In today's flattened organizational structure, employees make increasingly important business decisions every day—and they do it on their own. Each individual worker has the ability to set policy in ways that, though informal, are every bit as real as any 1400-page compliance manual—and carry a far greater potential for substantive change.

Of course, our values need to be aligned with those of the organization or else the situation simply won't be successful. A strong corporate culture drives real value. HR exhibits leadership when we make it possible to live the brand internally, reflecting corporate culture and reinforcing the brand consistently to external audiences. A sound structure and effective HR effort will provide individuals—and corporations—with increased resilience in a changing and stressful world.

I know that at my company, we're crystal clear about the value of a strong culture and a good working environment in which our people can thrive and excel. Ceridian's vision is to change the world of work, and our mission is to provide human resource solutions that maximize the value of people. You can't do that unless you take your own people—and your own leadership practices—dead seriously.

Every organization is an entity unto itself; each will have its own distinctive set of core values. If the organization can articulate these values clearly and continuously, it will attract, hold and motivate the kind of workers who share those values – exactly the kind of employees it needs to succeed. Never underestimate the power of values, and never underestimate the strength of individual effort. There is so much energy held within the workforce that corporate and personal values, when properly aligned, will unleash remarkable power.

HR must also have clarity around what we're bringing to the party. It is important that HR leaders not fall into the syndrome of feeling victimized by not having a significant voice in the organization. We need to possess the clarity to know what to say – and the courage to speak up and deliver the necessary message.

Other qualities necessary for an HR executive to succeed may be industry specific. In my industry, for instance, the modeling of HR strategies and HR leadership are an important part of the ideology. I have worked in several industries including financial services, high tech and educational software, and I've found that ideologies differ by industry. When I was in the educational software industry, the organization thought a lot about education and the training of employees because that was their value system. In high tech, we were driven by the idea of brilliance and expended effort to ensure that people had environments that supported their creativity. Within an HR solutions firm like Ceridian, it is about helping the organization understand the value of HR and to really step out and show what we have.

Strategies for Success

One strategy that I have developed is an approach I call "stealth HR." Stealth HR is the background work that gets done in order to position issues and plant ideas in the appropriate places – so that the ideas can take hold and really make a difference. Stealth HR is the way you can influence an organization, sometimes below the radar, until the time is right. Part of that is about championing top talent scattered across the organization. I'm not just being a cheerleader for them, I'm taking that network of people who have viewpoints, value systems, and ideas to contribute, and utilizing them in the stealth HR manner.

Another strategy is to always be checking in with my values and making sure that my actions are very consistent and values-based. Like any HR professional, I seek creative ways to manage challenge and to prepare for what comes next. Certainly consistency of action is required from anyone who works in HR, but it's especially important for senior HR leadership. There is no deficit of challenges for anyone operating in this field, and decisions of consequence must be made every day. Making those decisions comes down to integrity and having the courage to take actions that are values-based. When I use my talents and my resolve to help others, it enriches my life and my professional credibility. When I'm functioning as an arbiter of fairness within my organization, values are my fundamental guide. When I'm asked to align behavior with business values and corporate culture, there is a lot at stake—my instincts must prove fair and true. People watch closely, and interpret my actions.

The third strategy I use involves collaboration and partnering. To solve a problem within a complex system requires broader impact and perspective than any one function or person can apply. Teamwork and collaboration must start right from the top, and a key role of the HR executive is to foster this among members of the executive team. HR people seem to be "natural" team players, and can often serve as catalyst in the creation of meaningful collaboration.

Corporate organizational structure is no longer rigidly organized; instead, it is characterized by a fluid new dynamic, a culling of the brightest and a mixing of the best, with emphasis on cross-functional learning and strategic management of skill and talent. There is always something new to learn, and creativity is often sparked by new perspectives—but new knowledge and innovation require real dedication to sharing and cooperation. The more I learn about my organization, the more impressed I am with the caliber of the people who work within it. They are able to think creatively, to ask the provocative questions, and they manage cultural differences with grace and good humor. It would be impossible to do justice to the complexities of my corporate environment without close partnering and collaboration. My colleagues keep me informed and energized, and that keeps the fresh ideas coming.

Last is to always be forward-looking, always thinking about the future goals towards which we're striving. I look at how the steps we take today can help us to reach our future goals. Success is a process, an inexorable progression to the future. If we study well, the past guides us. If we trust our instincts, the present empowers us. When it comes to taking action, we look toward the future and powerful momentum is achieved. The pace quickens.

Changing Challenges

The most challenging aspects of human resources have changed. Ten years ago, the challenge would have been the need to prove our worth and get to the table. Then as organizations went through the era of belt-tightening and down-sizing, HR played such a key role that we were ushered directly to the table – for better or for worse. Now, the biggest challenge is resource levels; all functions are called upon to do more with less.

The U.S. has passed up Germany and Japan to become the single most productive nation on earth. We have reached this point partly through technology, but also as a result of putting more and more responsibility on fewer numbers of people. Organizations are increasing their productivity but not their head count. HR tends to be the place where companies are most fiscally conservative. In order to fund their product areas, customer-facing areas, and the other functional infrastructure groups that are seen as being more critical in delivering financial results, HR gets squeezed.

Overcoming this resource scarcity is really about using technology, looking at which activities can be outsourced, and looking seriously at process improvement. Do we really need to do all of the things that we're doing in the way that we're doing them? HR has become a lot more sophisticated about using techniques like Six Sigma and process mapping. HR professionals have become a lot more tech savvy as they search for resource saving alternatives.

HR has to leverage its impact, and can extend its capability when we invest in management and leadership development. In essence, every manager becomes his or her own "HR Manager;" managers can use one another as coaches and sounding boards, a role once reserved for HR.

HR Within the Organization

As head HR executive, I work with all of the executives in my company and therefore need to understand all of their positions. In my business, because we are a human resource solutions company, I work intensively with product management. Traditionally HR will partner tightly with corporate functional groups that are more governance-related, such as finance and legal. HR, finance and legal often form the solid "three-legged stool" that supports the CEO or president.

Members of the HR team must have a good sound theory base. They must possess depth in HR practices and philosophy. On top of that are other critical qualities: good judgment, a set of values that fits well with the organization, emotional intelligence and an orientation toward results.

Setting and Measuring Goals

We set goals as a team and our department goals flow from the business plan for the organization. This creates a cascading system that works down and bubbles back up again. It is a reiterative process until we've really honed in on the things that we need to do. People set their team goals based on what we've done at the HR level, and this cascading goes all the way down to the individual performance plane which then links all the way up.

With this process, we are given a clear line of sight on which we can report, and we can provide these reports on a regular basis. We are improving upon an HR dashboard, and the various functional entities within the company can establish metrics and statistics as well. We use soft reporting, too, to ensure that goals are met. People in the groups create monthly reports, and we also do operational reporting involving all members of the company management team on a monthly basis.

A key step in setting goals these days is to comb through and remove anything that's not completely necessary. We can't possibly tackle everything that there is to be done. Priority-setting and goal-setting are very real challenges in today's corporate environment. Because the trend in organizational structure is toward increased integration and fewer hard boundaries, the hierarchy is being broken down. Yesterday's tidy silos are disappearing fast. Some large organizations find it literally impossible to capture an accurate organizational chart because things are changing so quickly. In addition, the "do more with less" pressure means that we absolutely must find ways to cull out unnecessary or unprofitable effort.

The integration of work into daily living further affects the nature of the business environment – witness the impact of virtual workers, on-demand scheduling and the challenges of international time zones. Business' razor focus productivity has had strong effect. Now all eyes turn to HR strategy as a means of finding talent deep within the organization, a way to drive value by keeping everyone motivated and engaged.

The Changing Role of HR

If you go way back and look at the genesis of HR, there was a lot of focus on employee well-being. HR was born from a social work role that was played in the plants and factories of the last century. Over time, the HR function grew into the benefits area with welfare and fringe benefits, and has become increasingly integral to the operations of the business. We've moved from that pure employee advocacy caretaker role into a broader role. Certainly, the concept of change management and change leadership became a part of the HR function in the second half of this century and has gathered momentum in the last twenty years as everything has started moving faster in the world overall.

A new trend that is impacting us is healthcare. We've moved to much more strategic healthcare policy-making in the United States, and HR has had to get very creative on the benefits front. Employee benefits is an area where there is a huge focus on cost, but at the same time we are called upon to attract and retain employees – something that will be more difficult in the upcoming talent war.

Another focus for us right now surrounds the do-more-with-less trend. The need to do more with fewer resources impacts productivity and engagement. How much can you really push on people? The push for productivity in the workplace creates stress – and employee stress is a big issue all across the world, measurably impacting health care costs as well. Again, it is up to human resources to find a balance between pushing people and supporting them.

The shifting demographics are an area of pending change. As baby boomers begin to age, there are skill shortages starting to show already. Diversity is another element of demographics that's really followed social development in this country. We are looking at quite a different workforce in the future, and we're looking at huge shifts in terms of immigrant populations coming in as well. Trying to assess how that will impact our organizations in the future is a part of our changing role.

This idea of economic insecurity also plays out in the workplace. It feeds the productivity issues discussed earlier, because insecurity of this sort might cause people to hang onto their jobs when they normally wouldn't. Economic insecurity causes people to delay retirement; they're simply not retiring as soon as they once expected to. One result of economic insecurity can be a lack of trust around big institutions. There's a role for HR in establishing a work environment in which people can feel trust – and trust is a very rare commodity these days.

With the amount of change and challenge we face, it's critical to continually revisit our own sense of personal contribution, meaning and role definition. We have to remember why we chose the HR profession in the first place. For most of us, it's about making a difference in people's lives, in systemic ways. We want to make the world of work a better place for people. There is an incredible capability inside organizations to change the ways that people live. We affect our employees, their children and families for years to come. We can create legacies.

Working Culture

I don't believe that managers can be trained to inspire their employees. We have gone through an era of leadership development theory in which we discuss transformational, charismatic, and inspirational leaders—but at the end of the day, recent studies tell us that really good managers are humble. They're effective in ways that aren't always charismatic. It is hard to teach someone how to be humble.

Making Connections and Measuring Motivation

Employees will tell you when they are motivated and feel understood. You can measure productivity in the traditional ways, such as looking at measurements for revenue per employee, turnover statistics, and employee satisfaction metrics. Those things can be measured through surveys or focus groups. I feel the best way to measure employee happiness is by going out and talking with people as often as possible. It is important to have a system that encourages two-way dialogue.

What is really useful is to recognize that people do have lives outside of work, and that work-life balance is an especially important value for Generation X. Providing for balance in this area is important, since these individuals put purpose and passion in the same sphere as career. To this group, business success involves more than money; it involves doing work that is personally fulfilling and socially responsible. In the U.S. and around the globe, we are seeing job candidates who feel that it is impossible to have a meaningful life without meaningful work—and they will settle for nothing less. This is important for our very valuable older workers as well, for differing reasons. As Baby Boomers begin to retire and the job market tightens, employers must provide flexibility in the workplace and alternative schedules, so that people can make their own decisions about what works for them, including successively decreasing scheduled hours over time.

Humanizing the Workplace

Over the last couple of decades, organizations have begun to realize that people are the key to business; you can't treat people like machine parts. You treat people like human beings. This change in perspective has created a workplace that is more humanized. Communication and teamwork have opened up organizational systems considerably. Organizations see the results every day in higher levels of productivity and innovation.

Organizations are offering more and more flexibility to their employees, more and more services that allow people to balance work and family—and to be themselves in the work environment. There are other indications of humanization becoming apparent, too. I think diversity is one of those indications. We've seen an increase in representation from groups of people who previously weren't as well represented as they might have been, and it's made the workplace richer and more compassionate. All this makes work a more fulfilling place to be.

In addition, the rising costs of healthcare and the increasing importance of personal responsibility for retirement savings have forced some organizations to get really creative around their benefit plans. There is a limit to how much cost an employer can push off on employees, and so we're seeing a lot of effort put into employee education. There are new tools coming into the marketplace that help people better manage and better consume health care and plan better for their futures. In many ways, putting more control, more information, and more knowledge in the hands of employees is another humanizing step.

The HR Team

My team is motivated by the significance of making a difference. We are able to make that difference through planning, establishing what it is we're going to take on for the organization, and making sure that our linkage to the business plan is crystal clear and really tight. Putting a spotlight on some of the great work that people do is another way that department heads can inspire their employees. When we do our monthly operational reviews for the executive team, we don't just go through the statistics – we tell the story. I do a lot of crediting my team for their great ideas or giving them a showcase to stand up and present their own projects and their own work.

Employee Motivation

Our people expect financial reward. They expect to have parity with the market from a fairness point of view, but beyond that, they most value flexibility in terms of the ability to work from home and choose their own hours. They are also motivated by their relationship with their co-workers and with the customers they serve.

It is also important to recognize good work and effort. Having a variety of recognition vehicles is the way to ensure that a range of people receive rewards or acknowledgment. At Ceridian, we have various incentive programs in place, some that work across all groups and some that are specific to a particular function. A big piece of HR's role is to look across the organization and make sure that there is a sense of fairness and appropriateness around incentives, recognition and rewards. Different people and different types of functions have different needs.

We have implemented a peer-recognition program through which managers or peers can nominate people at a variety of levels for excellent work and for exemplifying our values and cultural tenets. Awards range from monetary rewards to a big trip at the end of the year. Every quarter we receive a number of nominations and each management team prioritizes who deserves to be recognized. We consider factors like who has received rewards in the past, the nature of each individual's work, and their alignment with our values.

We do a lot at Ceridian with events as well. If, for example, we're going to kick off a big project, we don't just have a meeting and tell everyone about it. We make it really fun with themes or costumes and different ways people can celebrate in the community. We try to include families with certain events such as our company picnics and holiday parties.

Measuring and Ensuring Productivity

Establishment of measures of excellence and personal development objectives are a critical element of performance discussions at Ceridian. Performance feedback communicates the individual's progress towards meeting objectives, and it documents the competencies attained as the person progresses. These reviews also serve to enhance work-oriented communications between the manager and the employee, reducing the likelihood of misunderstandings about responsibilities or expectations. Using this process, managers can provide each employee with a written review of demonstrated results against objectives. We make it clear that, although a partnership exists between the employee and the manager in the development and management of individual objectives, the employee is the ultimate owner of the objectives and of their own personal development.

In terms of increasing employee productivity, we do a lot with process improvement. We use Six Sigma methodology to look at processes and to analyze bottlenecks, remove unnecessary steps, or fix problems in our systems. This methodology is a discipline that forces us to analyze problems in various ways so that before we leap to a conclusion, we can be sure we've looked at all the factors, considered all the stake-holders, and examined the different outcomes. Six Sigma ensures that we understand the problem very well before we try to fix it, so that we aren't working on any assumptions.

Frequently, these process improvement initiatives are cross-group processes. We will pull a team together to work collaboratively. We take pains to ensure that the work itself is organized well and executed efficiently. We look at all our resources, considering tools and technology carefully so that we can ensure that people have what they need to get the job done.

Teamwork is another way to improve productivity. Because of the nature of business today, there is a high correlation between teamwork, cost containment and bottom-line impact. When an organization encourages employees to work together, rather than dictating actions from above, it creates a far greater potential for learning. Teams can address tactical and strategic issues in ways that are truly creative. They can find solutions to business challenges that might never be suggested in any other organizational scenario. Encouraging project-based learning through teamwork has a strong impact on productivity because the organization becomes more innovative and more effective. Individual management and leadership skills are enhanced. And cross-functional communication is encouraged throughout the enterprise. Besides, teaming reinforces relationship-building, and it's fun!

Creating a Culture of Productivity

It is important to have a culture that speaks to people, allows them to get excited about what they're doing, and gives them a connection to a sense of purpose. People give meaning to their experience and the information and knowledge they absorb. Each person creates their own context, applies their own values and layers in their own cultural interpretation. The potential to succeed in the marketplace depends upon an organization's ability to create common frameworks and contexts so that there is broad alignment of meaning and results. Because culture has strong potential to affect change, the value implications are broad.

By fostering the right corporate culture, organizations strengthen alignment without added expense, because culture can tangibly affect the behavior of their workforce. Because values like trust and honesty must be embraced deep within the enterprise if they are to be effective, this strategy shows strong potential for building integrity and trust in the eyes of shareholders and customers.

Organizations can respond to business challenges by creating and promoting a healthy corporate culture. For organizations everywhere, the new "leadership development" is *culture development*.

Related to culture is the concept of employment brand, or promise. A company's unique promise to its workforce takes on new cachet in a world dominated by the specter of a more competitive job market. And in the dynamic environment of global commerce, corporate leaders seek strategies that provide real returns and tactics that produce measurable results.

When the organization can live the brand internally and project it externally, it reflects the corporate culture consistently through people. A sound structure and effective communication effort provide individuals – and corporations – with increased resilience in a changing and challenging world. A strong corporate culture drives real value by motivating behavior and decisions that are "natural" and embedded in the fabric of the workforce.

Stress Management

Look at the realities of business today: employers push more and more responsibility on people who are already doing more with less. Sometimes these people are asked to perform without the tools and the support that enable them to fully succeed. The result? Added stress. Compromised productivity.

There are times when organizations make these pushes for productivity just because they must. There are restraints, and in those situations it is critical that everyone recognizes that they're in a crunch time. It's critical for leadership to demonstrate that they are appreciative for what people are experiencing. If you cross that line too often, though, employees will get over-stressed and their attitudes will shift. You need to make sure that you have the people in management and leadership roles who understand and care about issues of employee engagement and productivity.

Managing stress is serious business, because an engaged and motivated workforce is vital to corporate success. One way to help employees manage stress is through employee assistance and work-life programs. These solutions free the staff to focus on doing their best work. Work-life programs are an approach that keeps the organization competitive by creating a healthier, more effective workforce. The most effective solutions are those that allow employees to receive immediate, confidential access to help that gets them back on track. When workers can receive the kind of personal attention they need – when they need it – their stress is reduced. Their satisfaction rises. And their employer sees real impact in retention and productivity. By helping employees handle the issues that impact their lives, we can free the whole workforce to be more productive.

Another stress management strategy is surprisingly simple: have fun. Because human beings work, and because they are compelled to form relationships, there is nothing more satisfying than making a difference and having fun doing it with people we enjoy. This gets back again to the importance of corporate culture and its profound strategic effects. Ceridian is a good example of this. We discovered that as our corporate values began to resonate with our employees, they communicated their enthusiasm directly to customers in small but significant ways. Our customers responded in kind, and their feedback was so positive and so immediate that it was felt throughout the enterprise. The energy this created has been remarkable. It's really been quite an amazing thing to experience.

I believe that Ceridian's consistency of message has helped everyone in the organization understand the personal, business and professional value of their efforts. Our clear articulation of corporate culture has fostered a new appreciation for colleagues at all levels of the company – and a vibrant new connection with customers. We have engendered a work atmosphere that is more comfortable, more honorable and simply more fun.

Nancy Hanna, is Sr. Vice President, Human Resources for Ceridian Human Resource Solutions, an HR services and outsourcing organization headquartered in Minneapolis, Minnesota.

With over 25 years of HR experience, Ms. Hanna has a broad, global perspective on the changing world of work. Her background includes companies large and small, in industries including financial services and insurance, high-tech, and education.

Noted for her though leadership in the profession, Ms. Hanna speaks and writes on the role of HR, the changing world of work, and the development of high-performance cultures.

Ms. Hanna holds a B.A. in French, and an M.A. in Human Development.

She resides in Minneapolis with her family.

Getting it Right the First Time, Every Time

Ronnie D. Compton

Senior Vice President, Human Resources
Army Air Force Exchange Service

I am the Senior Vice President of Human Resources for the Army Air Force Exchange Service (AAFES). AAFES operates retail facilities on Army posts and Air Force bases world wide that provide goods and services to members of the military and their family. Profits from the sale of the goods and services are returned to the Army and Air Force as dividends to enhance the military members' quality of life by providing libraries, child care centers, gyms and other recreational activities.

AAFES grew out of the need to provide goods to the military member over and above what the government provided. Since there have been armies there have been merchants following and selling goods to the troops. It has been no different for the U.S. military. In colonial times and up though the late 1800s the goods being sold in many cases were so shoddy that soldiers were being taken advantage of. The practice reached such a state that on July 25, 1895 the War Department issued General Order number 46 directing post commanders to establish an exchange at every post where practicable. The general order set the standard for the concept and mission of today's exchange service.

Since the first formal exchanges were established in 1895, an exchange system has served side-by-side with Soldiers and, since 1947, Airmen in tents and trucks, in the field and in permanent facilities, on posts and bases around the world. From there it just grew to where we are today. We do almost $8 billion in sales and generate about $350 million a year that we give back to the Army and the Air Force based on the head count that they use for gymnasiums, for daycare centers, libraries, anything to do with an improvement of the quality of living of the soldiers. We get very little, or no money, from Congress. We are self-supporting but we have all the immunities and protections of a federal government agency.

As the Human Resources Director I am a civilian and I am one of thirteen senior executives running the different divisions. We are organized similarly to any large retailer. We have 47,000 employees and are commanded by a two star general with the second-in-command being a one star general. Our top civilian is the Chief Operating Officer. Our major divisions consist of Sales, Finance, Marketing, Logistics, Real Estate, Information Technology, and Human Resources and five sales regions: with three in the United States plus a region in the Pacific and one in Europe.

Direct Financial Impact and Adding Value for Your Company

Though our goals are always fluid, right now our main Human Resources goal is automation. By automation, we want to make the associate as self-sufficient as possible and to feel that all of us are working together regardless of the job. We have done that by enabling the associate to go on-line and make various changes, for example changes to a W-2, life insurance, change of address or to check their personnel record. The drive to automate reduces the number of people that I need. We are doing this to lower the cost for the delivery of HR services per head through automation we need fewer people. Another important goal is the unification of all of HR functions. I want to own all HR assets. Right now, I am the supervisor of all HR associates in the United States. The European and Pacific operation is supervised by the region chief who is the senior operator in that region. Although they follow the policies and procedures developed by the Headquarters they still answer to the region chief and not to me. The consolidation of all HR elements will ensure a consistent application of the rules and will bring some cost efficiency by reducing duplication of efforts.

Something that is unique to our organization is that we can only sell to a finite number of customers which are active duty and retired members of the military and their family members. We have to control our costs because we are not like Wal-Mart where we can build a new store and sell to anyone that walks in the door. Watching our costs is essential. I have to constantly monitor the number of associates. Since we're all over the world; we are constantly moving associates to new assignments especially overseas. Permanent moves cost us approximately $27,000 a move and I have to be in control of these moves to keep costs down. Another major thing affecting us financially as well as other retailers is benefit costs. Health care and retirement expense are two areas all retailers are going to have to deal with in the near future. Those are the big ones that have the greatest financial impact.

Creating Uniform Policies

AAFES is part of the Department of Defense, hence subject to many federal laws that don't necessarily apply to the private sector. In other words much of our policy is dictated by Congress. We do have leeway to develop internal policies that are consistent with law. We generally develop policy based on some need of the organization. For example, virtually all of our associates are civilians. However we operate worldwide. In order to get volunteers to serve in the far flung corners of the world we have to develop incentive packages that include benefits and monetary rewards. We do this centrally at the Headquarters but the policy is applicable to the entire organization. It is critical for any organization to have clear written policies and apply them uniformly throughout the organization.

The Art of Human Resources

The most important aspect of the art of human resources is to get it right the first time, every time. No matter how much information we put out the associate will still come to us rather than attempting to find the answer themselves. When people ask you a question you can't be wrong. It is a zero-defect job. We are not at that stage yet and nobody probably ever will be. We make mistakes but learn from every one of them. With the number of people we have in the organization it's so important to have the right answer for them every time.

Qualities of a Successful HR Executive

To be a successful HR executive you need to have a backbone of stainless steel. You've got to stand your ground. Many HR policies are not popular and you will be challenged. I'm not saying this in a negative sense it is simply the nature of the job. We are dealing with vast numbers of people and their lives are affected by policies and changes to that policy. It is critical not to take the criticism personally. You will not last long in this business if you do that.

You also need to deal even-handedly with people and not get in to any kind of favoritism. The associates expect that all the rules apply to all the people. If they find someone is getting favorable treatment your credibility is out the window.

Unique Aspects for the Human Resources Executive

Our single most unique factor is our current deployments. Each week we are sending associates to Iraq, where they are getting shot at, mortared and bombed. These are very tough deployments. The associates work 7 days a week and live in Spartan conditions. They support the military doing the fighting by providing goods and services for the service members. Our associates are volunteering to go for 6 months at a time. It is a unique operation to put a Burger King in Baghdad and get people to accept the position. What is surprising is that the people that go come back and say that it has been the most rewarding experience they've ever had in their life. We have been able to sustain 400 people at a time, "in the desert" as we call it, and people find it so satisfying to serve the troops that many volunteer to go back for a second tour.

Strategies That Make the HR Executive Successful

I have found that if you let your good people do their thing you are going to be successful. I manage four divisions. Our training branch "corporate university," is responsible for all training. We provide both internal instruction as well as sending our associates to outside courses. I have a "policy branch," which interprets the policy much of which is directed by the Department of Defense. We have an "operations branch," which handles all the field operations and issues. Finally, we have a "career management branch," which handles transfers, career progression and promotions. I give the four division chiefs I manage very broad guidance and then leave them alone. I do not believe in micro-managing. That is a concept so many executives fail to understand. It slows the process, creates stress and is inefficient. We have too many micro-managers in business. I tell my folks if they need a Senior Vice President to help them then I don't need them. I'll do it myself.

Overcoming the Challenges of an HR Executive

The most challenging thing I do is deliver bad news. Sometimes in this business you have to tell people unpleasant things. The key is to thoroughly explain the change and why. An example of this is the method we used in giving pay raises for promotion. When people got promoted

167

they got a 5 to 9 percent raise in their salary. Over time we realized this was too expensive and we needed to change the method. We made a change at the beginning of the year where the associate would get a one-time 5 percent lump sum for promotion although they could still earn annual pay raises based on their performance. We were asking people to take on a more difficult job but instead of their pay going up they would be given the lump sum. That was bad news. We needed to explain that we just couldn't afford doing things the old way.

We delivered this information by showing the dollars and cents of the situation. If we continued with the old system our personnel costs would soon exceed revenue which means you are broke. We could not waver on the implementation of the change. This is the way we are going to do it, and you've got to stick with it. I've told my people it's kind of like the grieving process over a loss experience. You tell them the policy and they go into denial for some time. Then they ask to bargain for some lesser policy. Next there is anger and despair. Why did this happen to me? Finally there is closure and hopefully acceptance of the loss. Throughout this process the HR executive has to remain firm with the employees and weather the storm.

Working Closely with Other Executives

I work most closely with the "region chiefs". As I mentioned before, we have five regions; three in the continental United States, one in Europe, and one in the Pacific. These chiefs are my counterparts and we are all the same rank/grade. The region chiefs oversee the store operations and the sale of the merchandise. My biggest challenge in dealing with them is providing them with the people **they** want in the stores. They are usually familiar with the candidates I propose to move to their operation. You may have to convince them that person who is next in line deserves to be promoted despite the region chief's assessment of their talent. It is a very intense process if one of my region chiefs does not want a specific person because the associates they get in the stores affect the region chief's career. I have to appreciate that the region chiefs are very successful and driven people and provide them the very best within the constrains of our policies. They on the other hand have to realize many of the moves are driven by promotion polices we have followed for years. Generally after several rounds of give and take we can reach an agreement, but sometimes it is stressful getting there.

Specific Skills for a Member of a Human Resources Team

The most important skills are interpersonal skills. I can teach anybody what the book says. I have staffed my senior level with people that can deal with people. I continue to direct my staff to look for interpersonal skills in a candidate first and we'll make them smart later. A person may be able to learn a job but if someone is annoying, cantankerous, or negative, you're dead. I have people that are happy, that are energetic, and that want to move the organization along.

Setting Goals and Checks and Balances for the Team

First of all, our goals come from the commander and they are typically financial goals because as a retail organization we're driven by earnings. Then each directorate such as Finance, Logistics, and Sales develop goals that support the corporate goals. Next the regions and ultimately the stores set goals to support the corporate goals. We have an automated system that provides the ability to determine the status of each corporate, directorate and region goal. It goes so far that each associate regardless of grade/rank must write goals. The goals are then measured at the end of the year and that's what their performance report and raise is based on.

The Future of Human Resources

I realize I may sound like a broken record, but I have to keep coming back to automation in predicting the future of human resources. When I started with the government, we did not have computers on our desks and personnel records were in hard copy. Now, everyone's personnel record is on-line and we don't have hard copies. An associate can sit down and punch up and look at their personnel record. We strive to automate everything that can possibly be automated. This has resulted in a significant reduction in the number of people that we need. On top of that, people previously had to leave their work stations, walk down to the personnel office and have the personnel manager complete even the simplest transaction such as a change of address. Now an associate can sit at their desk and make those changes in minutes. I kid my staff but my goal is to give the associate an HR pill in the morning and that's all the HR they will need all day.

Golden Rules for Human Resources

Of the golden rules for Human Resources, communication is probably at the top. There are so many rumors in a workplace that it's difficult to keep them under control. Usually about 20 percent of the rumors are correct, and the other 80 percent is a mix of several different all rolled together incorrectly. The more you can communicate, the better off you are. I've been at this for over 30 years. I enlisted in the military in 1967, so I've been working for the government for a long time, and there were always rumors. You're never going to stop rumors, but you have to be able to answer them, and the most effective way is face-to-face. Within my directorate, we have quarterly meetings with all the associates. We have a newsletter, *The HR Connection*, which contains HR articles of interest that goes to every associate. We're constantly in contact through email with our staff. Corporate-wise, the General has quarterly meetings; she presents them on TV and broadcasts it to the world. Typically the General, the Vice-Commander, and the Chief Operating Officer, will go on the TV together. People can send any question in on-line, about anything, and it'll be answered. They will take call-in questions, and if they can't answer them on the spot, we send them an email later. I think the key is to see management's face and to not beat around the bush, give it to them up front.

Work/Life Balance

To promote Work-Life Balance we have a very generous benefits package. Our leave package gives you thirteen days of paid vacation and sick leave a year to start, along with eleven paid holidays. After fifteen years, vacation leave increases to twenty-six days a year. We also have a very liberal flextime. Working with your supervisor, you can essentially come to work whenever you want. Certain operations are twenty-four hours a day, like our catalog center, call centers, and Information Technology which requires shift work. This gives the associate 3 different periods to work. Our regular staff has a work window between 6:30 a.m. to 8:30 a.m. and can come at any time. The single parent can work around any schedule and that is all a part of Work-Life Balance. We also have a free employee assistance program for any type of emotional problems. An employee can call up and get counseling. We try to provide for our employees and keep them happy and safe.

The Impact of Time Management

Time management is perhaps one of the most neglected concepts in business. Surprisingly small things can add up. For example, how often do you pick up the same piece of paper that requires action, how far you have to go to get something you have printed or how long do you let meetings run. Those are things I pay a lot of attention to. At our corporate university, we offer on-line courses on time management, classroom courses on time management, and the supervisors are always looking at how you're using your time. We are constantly training and looking for ways to do things more efficiency.

Measuring Employee Productivity

We measure employee productivity at the store level by taking the amount of sales and dividing that by the number of associates. That shows you what your productivity is per associate. If productivity gets too high you may have too few associates. If it gets too low you may have too many associates. Think about that. If you're doing a million dollars a day in sales and you've got one associate, productivity is a million dollars. If you have two, that's a half a million dollars. In retail too few associates can be just as damaging as too many. If you have too few you are probably losing sales. If you have too many your personnel costs are too high. We constantly struggle with getting just the right balance. We measure productivity for those not in selling positions generally by the goals developed between them and their supervisor at the beginning of the rating cycle. For example, the associate may pledge to process so many invoices for the rating period. At the end of the period that goal is measures. In all cases, productivity is a vital measure for the success of the business and the basis of rewarding performance.

Measurement and Benchmarking

Measuring and benchmarking is a fluid business. What is good today may not cut it tomorrow. We have a number of consultants that we contract with to provide us benchmarking data, and we measure against that. For example: I'm spending $550 per associate per year to deliver HR services right now. According to the benchmark data that is a little too high. I want something in the $400s based on the industry data and I am working now to reduce that cost. Measuring and benchmarking permits you to look at the things that are important and that you can change. It is surprising to find that you may not be doing everything as efficiently as you think.

Increasing Employee Productivity

As mentioned before, we measure productivity based on the sales per associate. Productivity as a general rule is best increased by plain old fashion motivation by management. Key to this is to show the associate what's in it for them. In most of our stores the number of hours available for the non management associates to work is based on sales. It sales go up they get more hours. It is important to explain this to the associate. When they understand that they will work to increase sales hence productivity. Another way to increase productivity is to find ways to get more of the customer's money. Add on is a popular way to do this. If you go into a McDonald's today, when the guy asks you if you wanted a pie with your order you don't think anything about it. However, that is a method that restaurants use to increase sales. You may not have even intended to buy a cherry pie, but he suggested it to you. He suggested to you not because he thought you wanted a cherry pie but because he wanted to increase sales.

Using the Internet and instant messenger has had a major impact on the administrative staff's productivity. When I came here in 1982, you wrote a letter and you waited two weeks for a reply or you made a phone call. In 1982 we had over 70,000 employees and now we've got 47,000. I attribute that reduction to automation because you can do so much more, over e-mail, internet and instant messaging. The key to success is always being on the look out for ways to do more with less.

The Tools of the HR team and Supervising Manager

The most essential tools in Human Resources are interpersonal skills. You're never going to beat that. I've seen brilliant people fail, and I've seen stupid people succeed because they can communicate with the people they are interacting with. People want to be communicated with and respected. Associates do not want to feel as if they are just cogs in a wheel. We have put new emphasis communication in the last couple years in an attempt to reduce stress and uncertainty. We have meetings where the associate has an open forum. We have a suggestion program. We have, not only the HR newsletter, but also a corporate newsletter, *The Exchange Post,* that goes out to all associates that contains articles about the business. However, I think the real action is with the lower level supervisor. That's going to make you or break you. I can have the grandest idea in the world, but if my front line associate doesn't execute then the idea is going no where. We have contracted with a company that provides us with a test that will indicate if a person is a happy person and deals well with others. You want someone that is satisfied with themselves, their lot in life, and the more of these types of people you can put into place; the more successful you're going to be.

Watching the Pitfalls

We need to be especially careful in watching for burn out when trying to increase employee productivity. We are constantly watching for overload. As humans you're going to come to some point where you cannot just keep working long hours. You have to watch for that overload period in the associate's behavior. We watch for the problem by tracking our workers' compensation claim "stress claims." Traditionally, we think of physical injury on the job as a workers' compensation claim. However, in recent history we are seeing associates file claims for mental anguish from on the job stress. Surprisingly, they are being successful in recovering compensation. When you start seeing people freaking out, you've got a problem. We carry about fifty "stress claims" at any given time. These are people at all levels, who just become overloaded. We have a full-time workers' comp staff, including a nurse that watches these cases. It's a delicate balance between pushing for productivity and taking care of the associate. There's no real good answer.

Sustaining Year-to-Year Gains in Employee Productivity

We have a unique benefit in serving the military. There is a lot of patriotism and that sustains productivity. One of our missions is to provide dividends to the military that enhance the members' quality of life and our associates really respond to that. When we tell them that we need to increase productivity four percent, they seem to do it. They seem to just go out there and do it because they really feel like they're doing something beyond working in the private sector retail where the profit goes to the stock holders. It is a commitment beyond just selling pots and pans, because they know the money that they're generating is going to go back to the soldiers and the airmen for worthwhile purposes. We rely a great deal on patriotism to sustain and improve productivity.

Incentives in Employee Productivity

Sales are the major unit of measurement used in assessing employee productivity and we use incentives to boost the productivity. We are somewhat different than the normal government agency that gives annual cost of living raises for just showing up. Previously, in our pay system we did that too. We have instituted a pay-for-performance system. Our performance scores range from 0 to 125 for our management people. We rank these scores by division from high to low. The top 10 percent get the biggest raise; the next 20 percent get the next highest, then the middle 55 percent, and the bottom 15 percent don't get anything. They don't get fired, but they don't get anything. So, last year, an employee could get up to a 9 percent raise, versus zero, which is an amazing performance award program. Those are the types of things that we're going to do to increase productivity. I've read the studies where people say the money's not that important but I believe it is. Every time you tinker with their money, you're going to hear about it. This was our first year using the new system and there was a great deal of what I call "gnashing of teeth." I told my staff, "You know Russia had a hard time going from the socialist system to a capitalist system, and it's going to be hard for us." It will take several years but in the long run business must be based on performance and not just showing up.

Supervisor Impact on Employee Productivity

The personal charisma of the lower level, front-line supervisor is one of the main impacts on employee productivity. If the person can have their team or their section feel like they're a group, they're making a meaningful contribution, and everybody's in it together, you are going to get good productivity. Invariably when the associate is complaining about the first line supervisor that section probably has productivity problems. You just can't be harsh to people and expect positive productivity. I tell the managers and those that are up-and-coming that "Your boss isn't the one that will cause you to get fired. It's the people that work for you in the end. So you better treat them right."

Productivity in the Coming Year

Across the board the retailer has to increase revenue plus control expenses or they will be out of business. It's a competitive industry. Productivity will increase by doing more with fewer people. You may never wind up with just one mega retailer but the number will certainly dwindle. Companies that are not increasing productivity, increasing sales and profits are going to go away. That is the challenge we all face.

Working at Capacity

Although the concept is a good idea, I'm not sure humans can work at capacity for extended periods of time. Business has to recognize this and determine how close to capacity they can get and still keep the person on the job. We have a computer system that tells us how many people you need in a store at any given time based on prior sales and customer traffic. The program then produces a recommended schedule. This is a step at determining the idea staff needed without over staffing. In the competitive market this is the type of steps that will be needed to keep the retailer in business.

Summary

If you don't like yourself, don't like others, and are generally an unhappy person, stay out of the HR business. For those of us in this business, we have got to continue to staff with people people! As staffs grow smaller it becomes even more important for every employee to be at the top of their game. HR work is fun; rewarding and you certainly will never have a boring work day.

Ronnie D. Compton is the Senior Vice President of Human Resources Directorate for the Army Air Force Exchange Service (AAFES) in Dallas, Texas. Mr. Compton is a 1975 graduate of Western Kentucky University with a B.A. degree, Summa Cum Laude in Political Science. He graduated in 1978 from the University Of Tennessee School Of Law with a Doctor of Jurisprudence degree. Mr. Compton received his Masters of Science degree in Human Relations and Business in May 2000 from Amberton University. He is also a graduate of the Air Force War College.

In 1982, Mr. Compton joined AAFES as an Assistant General Counsel at the Dallas Headquarters. In 1985, he was appointed as the AAFES Hearing Examiner responsible for hearing appeals of adverse disciplinary actions. He served as the Hearing Examiner until his transfer to the position of Deputy General Counsel, Europe in 1989. Mr. Compton returned from Europe in June 1993, and was appointed Deputy General Counsel for Employment and Labor Law. Mr. Compton was promoted to Senior Vice President, Human Resources in March 2003. Mr. Compton is a retired Air Force Reserve Colonel with more than thirty-four years of military service.

Note: The opinions presented in this chapter are exclusively those of the author and not AAFES, DOD or any other agency of the U.S. government.

HR: Mitigating Risk and Adding Value

Lawrence W. Hamilton

Senior Vice President of Human Resources
Tech Data Corporation

HR's Role

The role of Human Resources involves more than just one function. First, HR people are uniformly responsible for making sure the company that they are working with or working for is conforming to all the areas of legal compliance surrounding the workplace. These legal issues may relate to safety, health, affirmative action, equal employment and diversity, among other matters. The highly administrative record-keeping aspect of compliance is a large part of Human Resources as well.

The second value of Human Resources is a strategic focus in terms of how HR activities are programmed in order to mirror corporate strategy. Many more companies are spending greater amounts of time looking at competitive human resources practices involving recruitment and selection, development, assessment, and rewards and recognitions. For the most part, across all industries, people and people practices have a significant impact on of that firm's competitive advantage.

From the administrative, or back office, point of view, HR people are risk managers. We do our best to mitigate any risk that the organization may face as it relates to labor policies and practices, laws, and regulations. We potentially save the company millions of dollars annually by making sure we are compliant along local, state and federal laws that basically oversee people at work.

Another way that we add value is by implementing programs and plans to enhance the quality of the workplace and the employees. Among other programs, we establish performance management systems and develop competitive programs to pay and compensate talent as well as training and development programs to improve important skills. We ensure that the company has an effective leadership and employee satisfaction model.

HR practices are much like wall covered in different switches or levers. In certain combinations, these levers tend to make the organization as effective and productive as possible. The art of Human Resources involves understanding which levers and in what combination at what periods of time we need to activate in order to have the highest quality organization. With our access to all these levers, we determine what is the combination of activities, events, communication programs, etc. should be employed in order to most effectively utilize the human capital that we have so that the organization operates as productively as possible.

Addressing Issues: The Middle of the Road

HR people usually have the very uncomfortable task of sitting in the middle of the road. By practice, as opposed to definition, we are neither a full part of management nor a representative of management. We are neither a full part of the general employee population nor a representative of that population. Many would say we are asked to be the conscience and soul of the organization.

Our job is to assess, to a large degree, issues and items with which we are presented and to provide as best as we can the most objective view of what's right and what's wrong. There are many situations where we may completely take the employee's perspective and there are many situations we totally take the perspective of management. For the most part, HR people sit in this precarious place in the middle of the road where we can get hit by either side of the organization, whether it be management or people. We have to be comfortable with that level of flexibility and we have to have a high tolerance for ambiguity.

People issues are not spelled out necessarily in black and white. It's not like as strict as accounting or IT professions, where one knows what the rules or boundaries are and interprets within those boundaries. Dealing with the multitude of complexities that people bring into the workplace requires that we are prepared every day to encounter something that's totally different than what we thought it was going to be or have had to historically address.

Strategies for Success

Part of the HR person's career mission is to create an environment that drives employee satisfaction and engagement. We believe that if people are satisfied and engaged that they will provide us with that discretionary effort. They will go above and beyond the call of duty in satisfying our customers, whose purchases form us in turn will make our financial profile attractive and therefore make investors feel comfortable about investing. There is a linkage between how well employees feel treated and how that translates into customer activity.

We believe that people want to feel good about the company for which they work. The organization should have a good reputation as being credible, fair and consistent. Furthermore, it is important to instill a sense of affiliation and camaraderie, which we do by holding company-wide events such as banquets, recognition and awards events, and programs involving individuals, families and communities.

Employee satisfaction and engagement is strongly affected by a positive leadership environment. In our organization, our leadership principles are primarily related to developing performance, recruiting and retaining the top people, valuing diversity, and making a commitment to the organization. We promote self-development, professional development and community involvement because being a good leader means knowing who you are and how you impact people.

HR Skills

The head HR executive, in our organization, is a member of the Executive Committee and a member of the Worldwide Global Executive Committee. The position requires a high degree of interaction with out global president, our CEO and CFO. A head HR executive is very much a part of the company's business, so it is important that we know the basic tenants of the organization for which we work. We need to know, first and foremost, how our company makes money and the markets in which we compete. That awareness allows us to have a better impact on developing the human resource strategies that contribute to and impact the overall corporate strategy.

A member of the HR team needs to be busin ess savvy. He or she needs to possess a strong sense of self as well as excellent communications skills, both speaking and listening. Successful HR people need strong interpersonal skills, the ability to build relationships and value people, a high degree of commitment to their own development as well as the development of others, professionalism; adaptability, planning and execution and, most of all, they must have a strong judgment. They must have a strong focus in decision making qualities and business acumen.

Most of what we do is to determine objectively the next step in many processes. We have to decide what is the right thing to do in situations, which means being able to stand on our own two feet and not be swayed because we're interacting with the Chairman of the company or the Senior Vice President. If he or she is suggesting an action that we believe is not fair, it is incumbent on us to make sure we raise that issue and don't find ourselves on the outside looking in (or having to fix a bad situation).

Meeting Goals

At our company, every year our departments set their annual goals through a planning process called the AOP, an Annual Operating Plan or overall strategy. In that AOP process we identify what are the primary business drivers for that coming fiscal year. Generally the primary business driver will have some human aspect to it, whether it's acquiring talent, developing talent, purging talent, paying or rewarding talent or all of the above.

What is requested from the line to the human resources staff differs from year to year. With just over 8500 employees worldwide, there are some common practices we want to continue; there are others, of course that we do want to improve upon. Every department, function and country may have a different strategy given where they are in the continuum and where they want to move toward in terms of their human resource strategy.

Worst-Case Scenarios

Any activity that is related to any sort of legal violation (safety, EEO, ERISA) is probably the worst-case scenario given the amount of time and effort these types of inquires take. There is some level of disruption to an environment that eats very significantly into your available time and ultimately may eat away at the limited profitability that any business concern may enjoy. It is of utmost importance to build a work environment that allows associates to speak up about what they like and don't like about the work environment to develop healthy communication environment.

Budgeting Issues

Budget surprises can be prevented just by being very informed about budget expectations. Most mid-sized company HR budgets are in the millions of dollars range and are normally supported by many pages of actual detail behind each line items that provide very specific detail about our spending expectations. This detail helps stop surprises or, at the least, it aids in early identification of problems. If it seems like a budget problem is going to arise, it is best to let people know as soon as possible so that plans can be made for it.

We allocate a specific amount per each new hire, each training initiative and each salary. These budgets are rarely exceeded, and only fall short when we've had some unexpected turn over or we've planned for a particular level of job and we've had to go for a higher-level person.

Employee Terminations

If an employee must be let go, it should not be a surprise-not to either the employee or the supervising manager. With our AOP, Annual Operating Plan, we establish goals that are divided into intermediate or specific goals for the executives and for the staff. We model our employees' goals and their performances against these goals, so we generally know whether someone is or is not performing up to the corporations overall plan.

In the situations where there is a performance problem, we use a formal system that first starts with a verbal discussion and then if the performance doesn't continue to hit the expectation, we document that issue in writing along with a developmental plan to assist the employee in developing the desirable actions to close the performance gap. We have final written documentation before someone is released. We take these steps as a way to provide fairness to the individual so she/he has an appropriate level of due process but also are given an opportunity to improve. We want to make sure people have an opportunity to voice their concerns, and in most cases, the Human Resource person is right in the middle of that process.

Hiring

We think that non-management positions should be filled within 45 days or less while positions that are management or above should be filled in 60 days or less. Technological advances have increased the number of available hires because we can pull qualified candidate resumes off internet-based employment boards and postings. The high use of temporary employees also raises numbers, as does the amount of people who are interested in part-time work. Demographic reports indicate that as the baby boom population continues to age, they may look at their quality of work and outside-work life, and decide to work less or not at all. Businesses may begin to rearrange work around our available resources and the expectations of multiple generations in the work force.

The challenge unique to hiring C-level executives is finding the right candidate mix and making sure that they represent the functional expertise that they say they do. We have to ensure that they fit our culture. There's nothing worse than hiring someone at the C level who turns over or leaves in a short period of time because we have wasted a good deal of time, effort, money and investment in that person.

I think this whole idea of generations in the work place is going to probably be a lot more important in the future. I think the economy is going to pick up a bit, so we're going to see some growth in the marketplace, and therefore there will be many opportunities to look at who is being recruited, who is being let go, what skill sets are missing and other major shifts.

Employee Loyalty

Leadership

Loyalty is driven by a variety of things, but one of the key forces behind it is really solid leadership. HR people have a responsibility to really help develop leaders and instill employee pride in the company. A platform of affiliation, camaraderie, ethics and values is reinforced by positive leaders. These leaders need to be role models who people trust, respect and feel possess a sense of consistency and credibility-they do what they say and do it consistently every time. People can feel like they can trust their management team and have consistent outcomes. They are the primary representatives of the policy-making branch and the company. If leaders don't demonstrate these ideal qualities, then they are unlikely to be consistent throughout the organization.

For any relationship, whether it's romantic or friendship or professional, it's often the little things that count. Many of the same tenants that you find in interpersonal relationships, the one-to-one, are represented in a one-to-many relationship in an organization. If a supervisor promises something, such as a promotion or a pay increase, he has to come through. If a supervisor talks to his employees, even offers to pick someone up a cup of coffee when he's going out, small gestures like that will make a big difference.

Benefits

The importance of benefits in fostering employee loyalty depends. The younger the employee, the less he or she really cares about certain fringe benefits. It seems like our younger employees want benefits that are portable. They're not looking for a retirement plan, they're looking for a 401K with huge match. They don't care about having a huge life insurance plan, because they can't take it with them. More mature employees are looking for a bit more security (retirement savings and medical plans). They are concerned about their medical benefit costs because they want to make sure that they're going to have benefits to take care not only of their kids, but also themselves as they grow older.

Lawrence W. Hamilton, SPHR/CCP, is senior vice president human resources, a corporate officer and member of the Executive Committee at Tech Data Corporation in Clearwater, Florida. Mr. Hamilton joined Tech Data in 1993 as Vice President, Human Resources and was named Senior Vice President, Human Resources in 1996.

Prior to joining Tech Data in 1993, Mr. Hamilton served in a variety of human resource management positions with Bristol-Myers Squibb Company in Evansville, Indiana, New York, New York and Largo, Florida during the period of 1985-1993. Most recently, between 1991 and 1993, he was Vice President, Human Resources and Administration at Linvatec, a subsidiary of Bristol-Myers Squibb in Largo, Florida.

Lawrence received a BA degree from Fisk University (cum laude) and an MPA from the University of Alabama where he was an American Political Science Association funded Fellow. He is a certified Senior Professional in Human Resources and recently received the CCP designation (Certified Compensation Professional) from the American Compensation Association. He is presently attending The George Washington University as a doctoral candidate in the Executive Leadership Program with a concentration in Human Resource Development. He completed the academic coursework and comprehensive examination requirements for the program in June 2002 and is presently in the dissertation phase of the program.

In addition, Mr. Hamilton has served as past President of the INROADS/Tampa Bay, Inc. Policy Board of Directors and is an at- large representative on the INROADS, Inc. Board of Directors. He was Secretary of the Board of Directors for Junior Achievement of the Suncoast, Inc. and served as Chairman of the Human Resources Committee and a member of the Board of Directors of the Long Center (Clearwater). He is presently a member of the PRIDE, Inc., Board of Directors and involved in a host of other professional and community-related activities and organizations. He is also a Life Member of both the Fisk University Alumni Association and Kappa Alpha Psi Fraternity, Inc. He is married to the former Karen E. Fraction, an actress, and together they have two children-Lauren (age 12) and Lawrence Wm. (age 6).

Aligning Business Goals with Management Philosophies

Robert Lincoln, Jr.
Senior Vice President of Global Human Resources
Manpower, Inc.

HR Goals and Skills

Human Resources is the group responsible for developing and implementing the processes, policies and strategies that create a human organization capable of winning in the marketplace. My role is to develop and implement human resources strategies that will globally leverage HR policies and practices while contributing to the success of the business. The tools to achieve this broad, global goal involve compensation & benefits, talent management, performance management and succession planning. The policies developed in these areas have a direct impact on the financial success and value of my company. The three biggest things are:

- Succession Planning
- Performance Management
- Employee/Management Development

The Human Resources function is the group responsible for developing, acquiring and implementing the processes, policies, technologies and strategies that create the human organization that is capable of winning in the marketplace.

The successful HR executive needs to:

Understand how to manage and lead the HR function in any industry. The HR Executive has to harness his accumulated knowledge and apply it to a variety of business and industry environments In order to do this successfully, there are other qualities that the HR Executive must possess.

Understand the business drivers in their industry. While the work of Human Resources is transferable to any industry, there are unique business drivers that must be understood by the HR Executive to ensure that the human organization being created will be successful in the marketplace, in the particular industry. Accordingly, it is imperative that the HR Executive network internally and externally to have an accurate and contemporary perspective of the business drivers in the particular industry, and their current and future ramifications on people issues within the company. This understanding becomes the cornerstone for the development of the companies Human Resources Strategy.

Be philosophically aligned with the CEO. At this level, the "work" of leading the HR function can be accomplished by a number of senior level professionals but the most critical qualification is the philosophical alignment with the CEO. This is important because the CEO's HR philosophy will determine how much latitude the HR Executive will have in creating and developing the function, and what the people policies and practices of the company will be.

Have the human, organizational and financial resources that will ensure the successful accomplishment of goals. Having experience and being philosophically in sync with the CEO are key enablers of success for the HR Executive. However, these characteristics are sub-optimized if the HR Executive is not provided with adequate resources (and time) to achieve the people related goals of the organization.

Have courage. Often the nature of HR decisions are difficult because they impact the livelihoods of large numbers of people. Additionally, the cost implications of HR decisions have ramifications that can dramatically impact profits. The competence to determine which decisions must be made is negated unless the HR Executive has the courage to actually make decisions and the conviction to stand by them.

Have vision and the willingness to implement that vision. The successful HR Executive always has a strong sense of what possibilities are and how to begin to achieve those possibilities.

HR in the Staffing Industry

The prevalent ideology in the staffing industry is, "We put people to work!" In other words, other industries employ people for their own purposes. The staffing industry employs people for other people. Accordingly, there is a belief within this industry that our business benefits the greater good and not just ourselves.

I maintain an external network of HR professionals upon whom I rely to keep me grounded. I talk with them about issues that I'm dealing with on the job (boss, coworkers, and subordinates) and use them as sounding boards for proposed solutions. From them I receive objective, direct feedback that I value. Since they are not working for me (and vice versa), we can be completely candid without fear of professional consequences or retaliation.

Overcoming HR Challenges

Historically, the most challenging aspect of being in HR is that managers in other functions or businesses believe that they can "do HR work," and/or "HR isn't necessary." The best way to overcome this obstacle is to educate managers about the role of contemporary HR. We also try to show them what the HR function is or could be capable of accomplishing if it is given a broader role in the organization.

The other challenge in HR is being tasked with surmountable goals by the organization, but not having adequate resources to achieve the goals. To address this problem, we show management how we could drive business success if given more resources. We demonstrate how these resources could also reduce costs. This is achieved both through presentation to management on theoretical examples and actual job performance by HR professionals in the workplace.

Most of my contact is with the CEO, CFO, CIO and Business Vice-presidents. It's important for me to understand their roles in the organization, what their goals are, what they perceive the strengths and weaknesses of HR to be, and how they want HR to interact with them and their respective areas of responsibility.

When working with these figures, I believe that establishing a mutual understanding of what success looks like is important. That way, alignment between HR deliverables and business success can be agreed upon. Also, obtaining a commitment that cooperation is mutual is essential. I worked in an organization where the boss demanded flawless delivery of HR systems, but did not demand flawless cooperation from our clients. This philosophy was unsuccessful because it did not facilitate engagement and ownership from the client, thus setting up the HR function for failure.

The HR Team

In the twenty-first century, the HR professional needs to be:

Technically Proficient - Given the technical and diverse demands of HR, the individual must be technically proficient in HR in order to be effective and successful. Being a "people person," or a "good fit for HR," no longer guarantee entrance to the human resources function.

Excellent Communicator - The complexities of people issues and the changing needs of business make above-average written and spoken communication skills mandatory for today's HR professional who must be able to regularly articulate HR strategy and systems to Boards, management and employees.

Courageous - The ability and willingness to take positions, offer perspectives, and take risks that enhance the human organization and support business success will make the HR professional a valuable business partner and employee advocate.

Team Player - Having a viable role on the team, combined with the resources to effectively contribute to the goals of the team allows the HR professional to be a successful team player.

Confidant - Confidentiality is the cornerstone of the HR profession. However, having access to confidential information through the course of one's job duties and having employees purposefully seek you out to discuss confidential matters are two different things. The ability to have the ear of a company's leadership, be the conscience of management, and the advocate of employees is an acquired skill, rather than implied one. The successful HR professional in an individual who has the capability of acquiring this skill.

Visionary - Having a sense of what the HR function can do, given the nature and scope of the business, coupled with external market trends, internal cultural and organizational capabilities & limitations will enable the HR professional to develop a meaningful vision that will facilitate employee productivity and development.

Strategic - The HR professional must be able to successfully implement and align the tactical elements of their vision as a comprehensive HR strategy.

Business Acumen - The HR professional must possess a reasonable business knowledge to be able to understand the fundamental principles of business and apply them in the development and implementation of HR strategies. It is not necessary for the individual to be business professional in order to be a successful HR professional.

Goals within the HR team are driven from the top down and are influenced by function and business. The HR goals are aligned with the "people related" goals of the CEO. There are also people goals from the businesses and other support functions that need to be included in the goals of the larger HR function. Everything we do revolves around business alignment and relevance to business success. Our checks and balances come in the form of quarterly goal review sessions and two-level review in which the boss's boss reviews the goals as well.

The Present and Future of HR

HR has moved from being a Low Tech employee driven "Personnel" function, to being a High Touch "Employee Relations" function. Historically, companies had large numbers of HR employees who had responsibility for doing all of the "people" things. In some cases, this involved not only compensation, benefits, staffing, recruiting and training, but also included such mundane tasks as planning office parties and retirement parties. The HR function was primarily an administrative function who did things for employees. Hence, it was "high touch." Very little computer automation was employed by HR to accomplish these tasks (thus the "low tech" label). During the late 80's and early 90's, employee downsizings turned HR into a Low Touch function.

The HR function had moved from doing thing "for" people to having the reputation for doing things "to" people. Needless to say, this resulted in HR having diminished credibility with employees and consequently losing a great deal of the institutional capital it had built up. The Internet boom made the function become more High Tech by using computers to streamline benefits enrollment, deliver online training, allow managers to directly input compensation changes, and automate recruiting and succession planning. Some of these gains were achieved at the expense of becoming "No Touch" in the quest to be a "Business Partner." The technological improvements gave HR more credibility with management, but it resulted in fewer HR people to work directly with employees. The value of the Business Partner relationship was that it made the HR Function more Process Driven and this in many cases allowed HR to establish the "Right Touch" within various companies. Having learned from these past successes and mistakes, HR today is constantly looking at the Right Processes and the Right Technology at the Right Price. The current HR professional knows that there is a balance that must be achieved between process, technology, and people deployment, and that there are cost considerations that must be understood and addressed.

I believe that the next evolution for HR will be a return to Employee Advocacy, previously the domain of HR, but suppressed because of fear of downsizing, outsourcing, and not being "asked" to be a "Business Partner." The reason for the return to Employee Advocacy will be because of the need to sustain employee loyalty in the workplace. As the available, qualified labor pool continues to shrink, the competitive advantage for a corporation will lie not in it's products and processes, but rather in innovation and productivity to be sustained and improved as a result of a well trained, consistent, dependable workforce. It is this workforce, which is knowledge-based in the industry, in the company, in the culture, which will enable it to defeat in the marketplace companies with high turnover, transient employees.

HR Golden Rules

Remember that HR is a "service" organization, not a "servant" organization. The purpose of the HR function is to possess, develop and implement the technologies and strategies that assist management in creating the human organization that is capable of winning in the marketplace. This means that the function doesn't exist merely do what they're told by management to do, rather, they are, as a result of analysis, technology, expertise and confidence, providing advice and recommendations that will enable business success. The HR function has to be dynamic, agile and engaged in decisions, before "final plans" are implemented by the business.

Acknowledge that the people who pay the bills don't always do what is best, long-term, for the people who do the work. The greatest challenge for HR is to facilitate the holistic understanding of management of the ramifications of business decisions on people decisions. This means that business decisions that result in profits for the next quarter might create problems for employees for years to come. This is not to suggest that management intentionally and routinely make decisions that adversely impact people, but it does suggest that there is always a possibility that any business decision could adversely impact people. Having a holistic understanding of the consequences of decisions on people, and a plan of action to deal with the consequences, is a barometer that separates great companies from good companies. The desired role for HR is to partner with management in such a way that the human consequences of financial decisions are discussed, understood and communicated appropriately.

Perform your job in such a way that rules #1 and #2 aren't conflicting, but are complementary and contribute to employee satisfaction, customer satisfaction, and business success. The HR function cannot afford to be delusional about the realities of the above-mentioned golden rules. Instead, the function has to be prepared to address the myriad of contingencies that result from these rules, and do so in a productive, constructive, non-threatening, non-defensive manner.

Potential HR Nightmares

The human resources strategy has to align with the goals of the business and the p hilosophy of management; otherwise, a nightmare will occur.

The worst possible scenarios that HR has to deal with are:

That HR isn't "at the table" with management. This means that the culture of the company and the mindset of management is such that HR is not a valued function, and is neither seen as nor wanted as a member of the business team. This can be prevented by establishing the need for HR at the table, and by quickly and consistently demonstrating the value that HR adds by being part of the business team.

That the HR function has decentralized process and practices. This means that HR is run geographically by autonomous HR leaders who don't communicate with each other and who create different processes and practices and policies for "people things" that should be common throughout the company. The result is duplicative costs and redundant activities that compound inefficiencies because rarely are internal or external "Best practices" employed in an environment where they have not previously been communicated or rewarded. This can be prevented by having clearly understood roles and responsibilities for geography's and functions.

That the HR function is outsourced and managed by a third-party consulting firm. This means that the HR professionals within the company have their employment terminated and they are either replaced by a third-party firm who performs the HR work, or they (the HR Professionals) join the third-party firm and perform the HR work. While there are short-term financial efficiencies gained, what is lost, long-term, is the cultural and institutional knowledge that the HR people have about the day-to-day "pulse" of the company. Employee advocacy is diminished, and ultimately, so is employee satisfaction and correspondingly, customer satisfaction.

Budget Issues

Establishing budget compliance as a performance goal for individuals is the best way to prevent budget surprises. Department heads are responsible for establishing budgets based on what they are going to accomplish in the coming year. If they accomplish the goal, but exceed the budget, there are consequences to their variable pay and future opportunities. If they don't accomplish the goal but stay within the budget, there are consequences to their variable pay and future opportunities.

Terminations and Hires

The amount of time it takes to fill a position depends on many factors. If the position is senior and critical to the organization, succession planning should play a key role. Ideally, there should be a candidate (or candidates) to fill every critical role and every management role in the organization. In the absence of candidates, there should be a known and documented process to acquire new candidates. While time is always of the essence, it's more important to select and obtain the right person for the job, rather than filling it quickly. How fast a job should be filled varies from one corporate culture to another.

Benchmarking Success

I believe that an HR Department should benchmark itself against where it was and where it wants to be as the first and primary measure of success. It should be assumed that "where it wants to be," has been determined by working with management and is aligned with the direction of the business. External benchmarking is fine within the same industry and broadly, but unless you're tying to become the twin of another company that brand of benchmarking has diminutive value.

HR and Other Departments

There should be an HR professional assigned to/aligned with every department/function/business within a company. In that way, HR can consistently deliver services to those departments, and develop an understanding of their unique needs and strategic direction. One HR person can be aligned with several departments as part of their job duties. The key is to put the right number of HR people against those departments who really need it, as opposed to establishing a blanket ratio of HR people to employees, the way that many companies do.

For example, through benchmarking, a company might become aware that a select group of "top performing companies" have a ratio of 1 HR professional for every 1,000 employees (1:1000). As a result, they restructure their HR function so that they have the same ratio. The problem with this approach is doesn't take into consideration that all functions and business units within a company are not equal in terms of their HR needs and usage. By way of illustration: One group within the company might be in the process of downsizing, while another is in the process of acquiring a new business. Another group might have a more mature, experienced workforce, and yet another group might be in startup mode and have newer employees with more contemporary skills, but less work experience. The point being that while each of these groups undoubtedly have shared Human Resources needs, they clearly have unique people needs that impact their businesses and functions. The shared HR needs can be leveraged and delivered tactically. The unique needs must be understood on a group basis, delivered strategically, and resourced according to the priorities and needs of the overall company business strategy. Accordingly, HR has to be organizationally flexible and agile in order to align the best number (and skills) of HR professionals to meet the needs of the business. A rigid adherence to a service ratio that may or may not be transferable from one company to another will limit the effectiveness of delivering HR services.

Preventing Nightmares

The best way that HR can prevent future nightmares is through preparation. HR Professionals must be technically proficient, well-educated, and trained in the culture and politics of their company. There must be a realistic understanding of

- what the company is,
- what it thinks it is, and
- what it aspires to be.

HR will have to work in each of these three realms in order to contribute to business success.

In order to successfully deal with HR nightmares, there has to be flawless cooperation between HR and Management. In order for this to occur, HR and Management should establish internal service agreements and communicate these to employees so that all parties can actively contribute to the success of the necessary partnership between HR and Management.

Robert W. Lincoln, Jr., was the first ever Senior Vice President of Global Human Resources for Manpower Inc., headquartered in Milwaukee, Wisconsin. Lincoln has over 25 years of experience in Human Resources Management and people strategy development and implementation. Before joining Manpower in 2002, he formed Robert Lincoln Consulting, LLC, a firm specializing in strategic human resources planning, change management, cultural integration and the coaching and counseling of executives, people managers and Human Resource professionals. He was previously the Global

Director of Human Resources, Mergers and Acquisitions, for The Dow Chemical Company, located in Midland, Michigan.

Mr. Lincoln is a graduate of Michigan State University, where he received Bachelor's and Master's degrees in Psychology and Counseling. He also has a Juris Doctor degree from the University of Houston. He is certified by the Society of Human Resources Management (SHRM) as a Senior Professional in Human Resources (SPHR). An active speaker on human resources issues, Mr. Lincoln has addressed numerous audiences in Europe, Latin America, South Africa and Asia, in addition to North America. His publications include the article "Dealing with HR Issues following the 9/11 Terrorist Attacks" featured in Employment Relations Today, Winter 2002, and the book, "100 Things To Do If You're Downsized," released in July 2002. He has developed a companion seminar, "Downsizing: Principles, Practices and Procedures," for The Human Resources Education & Training Center, School of Labor and Industrial Relations, at Michigan State University. In June 2003, he attended the inaugural session of the Chief Human Resources Academy, sponsored by the National Academy of Human Resources Foundation. In December 2003, he was elected to the Advisory Board of the Medical College of Wisconsin Cardiovascular Center. In March 2004, he was elected to the Board of Directors of the Human Resources Policy Association. Lincoln was also member of the 2004 World Economic Forum panel, "Do Labour Rights Partnerships Work?"

HR as a Strategic Partner

Anne Donovan Bodnar

Managing Director, Human Resources
Towers Perrin

The Role of HR

The role of human resources has changed enormously in the past five years in virtually every organization, and Towers Perrin has been no exception. We are a global professional services firm, and a significant part of our business consults with HR leaders at some of the largest companies in the world. It is not surprising, then, that our firm's leadership, with its deep expertise and extensive client experience, sets high expectations for the delivery and management of its own internal HR services.

The primary goal of the HR function at Towers Perrin is to ensure that the firm's HR programs and processes are optimally aligned to help the business attract, develop, engage and retain the talent we need to serve our clients. Many HR people (and many of our consultants) would call this being a "strategic partner" to leadership. It's hard to argue with this—who wouldn't want to be labeled "strategic"? —but it somehow creates the misleading impression that the operations and administration areas of HR don't count. You only have to be on the receiving end of a call from an employee with a chronically ill child whose claims have been mishandled to get this point. In fact, the pressure on HR to provide high-quality, cost-efficient delivery is relentless and will remain so. My belief is that in order to become a strategic partner for the business, HR needs to tend to the business of HR—and that means not losing sight of the importance of process design and execution. The need for more streamlined services has never been greater, and given the highly competitive nature of the global economy, this need is unlikely to relent any time soon.

For us, that has meant tackling everything from an overhaul of our entire rewards approach globally to revamping our HR information systems to redesigning our international transfer policies—all during a time of extraordinary change and challenge for our firm and our industry.

Finally, I'm not sure the word "strategic" fully encompasses one of the most critical roles of the HR function: to serve as the workplace conscience of the organization and its leadership. As decisions are weighed and alternatives are balanced, HR leadership must advise management on the extent to which certain courses of action support the organization's values. This is particularly true in an era when corporations, their leaders, and the advisors who serve them are under increasing scrutiny. I feel fortunate to work with a CEO and a senior leadership group that has demonstrated an uncompromising commitment to the most ethical and principled courses of action. This has meant working with our leadership on some very difficult decisions on people issues, business issues, and even client matters.

There is no argument that HR should play the role of a strategic partner to management. A number of compelling factors have emerged in the last several years to move the HR function from a relatively back-office operation to one that plays—or should play—a critical role in an organization's success.

Competition: Setting High Standards

First, the nature of business itself has changed dramatically. Competition has intensified to the point that a new concept or product, once introduced by a company, has a shorter and shorter life before it is replicated—often at a lower cost or with additional features—by a competitor. So companies innovate at a faster pace than ever before. As a result, they increasingly rely on their people as the key competitive differentiator.

As former secretary of labor Robert Reich says in his 2002 book, *The Future of Success: Working and Living in the New Economy,* "The more intense the competition to offer better products and services, the greater the demand for people with insights and ideas about how to do so."

My own firm is a case in point. We don't manufacture products or offer consumer-based services, but we operate in an extremely competitive business-to-business market. All of our success rests on our people, on their technical skills, and on their ability to develop new ways to help our clients succeed. We rely on them to do much more than merely show up every mornin g. We count on them to be actively engaged in our business and to give that extra bit of effort that makes the difference to our clients. In short, people are the engine that drives our financial and operational performance. We expect them to help us deliver on our mission, which is "to make significant contributions to improving our clients' business performance through our unique combination of talent, expertise, and commitment, thereby creating value for our stakeholders." And to deliver on our vision, which is "to be a preeminent global firm that the business and professional communities hold in the highest regard. We will achieve:

- Marketplace leadership by building businesses with best-in-class capabilities to deliver measurable results for our clients
- Workplace leadership by building a community of exceptional professionals who, individually and collectively, want to contribute to and be part of a high-performance organization."

We also expect our employees to live by our values, which are "the values of integrity, respect, and professionalism. We embrace such attributes as agility, innovation, high performance, and discipline that, in combination with our values, will help us realize our vision."

In other words, our clients expect big things from us, and we expect just as much from our employees. Our own Towers Perrin research has shown a linkage between employee behavior, customer satisfaction, and business performance. And employee behavior is driven by people programs and services.

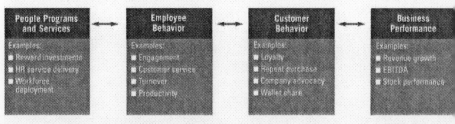

It is my job as head of the HR function to ensure that we help the business find, retain and develop people willing to put forth the discretionary effort that ensures the success of Towers Perrin and our clients.

Hires

At Towers Perrin, the kind of people we look to hire and develop are intelligent, high achievers, who come with a strong internal drive and capacity to learn and grow. In short, we have terrific raw material.

Even so, as a general rule, employee discretionary effort doesn't just happen. It is determined by a number of factors that my colleagues at Towers Perrin have identified in the course of their work and that we use to help other organizations drive their own performance.

What are the factors that drive employee engagement? Our HR Services business conducted a 2003 talent survey, "Working Today: Understanding What Drives Employee Engagement" which has provided important insights about this question.

Unfortunately, of the forty thousand employees of large U.S. and Canadian companies that responded to our survey, only 19 percent said they are highly engaged in their work, and 64 percent said they are moderately engaged. When we look at the top-ranked engagement drivers, only 42 percent rated their companies favorably on "senior management has an interest in employees' well-being," only 34 percent were favorable on "employees have excellent career opportunities," and only 45 percent were favorable on "senior management communicates clear vision for long-term success."

Employee respondents said that the top drivers of engagement are the following, in order of importance:
- Senior management's interest in employee well-being
- Challenging work
- Decision-making authority
- Evidence that the company is focused on its customers
- Career advancement opportunities
- The company's reputation as a good employer
- A collaborative environment in which people work well in teams
- Resources to get the job done
- Input on decision making

- A clear vision from senior management about the future success of the organization

Interestingly, salary and benefits are *not* among the top engagement drivers, but make no mistake: they are what we call "needed to play" elements. That is, an organization simply cannot hire and keep top talent without providing market-competitive salaries and benefits. However, once employees are on board, they look to engagement drivers to keep them motivated, directed, and giving their best.

Employees have told us which factors drive their engagement, and they've also said that, by and large, their companies are not paying enough attention to these factors. There is enormous opportunity here for HR. We are in a position to influence many of these factors from a program and process design point of view, in areas such as organizational communication, career planning and management, rewards and recognition, and a respectful work environment. But here is where the partner concept is so critical. HR alone cannot succeed in raising employee engagement; it must work closely with the business leadership to bring the policies to life in the workplace. HR can provide the expertise and the design, but leadership must provide the commitment to making the programs work.

Acknowledging Current Realities

A handful of important business realities currently affect our business. Among them are the following:

Employment markets have changed significantly. The overheated market for talent that existed in the late 1990s is gone, and companies are operating ever leaner and expect more from their staff. In addition, the tougher economic climate and the sense of political uncertainty post 9-11 have further accelerated the evolution of the relationship between employee and employer in virtually every organization. While many individuals value stability or security, overall employee expectations have changed dramatically. The successful firm today emphasizes development, challenge, and opportunity for reward, rather than stability or job security. At Towers Perrin we expect our employees to keep their technical skills current, to maintain computer and other technology skills, and to keep abreast of trends in key industries, such as insurance and financial services, which are important segments for our firm. In many of our businesses, we are sought out by global corporations and by regulatory authorities as thought leaders on risk, benefits, compensation and many other topics. This means that we need to attract and retain people who are considered to be the absolute best of the best in their profession globally. Because we hire across the world in many different talent areas, we find some parts of our business competing in tight labor markets, with intense recruiting cycles and high demand for a limited pool of talent, while other parts of our business are faced with lower demand for services, resulting in low hiring rates, low rates of voluntary attrition, and a shift toward increased involuntary attrition. What's more, the definition of "employee" has grown more complex. At Towers Perrin, for example, in addition to regular full-time employees, we work with vendors' employees, freelancers, and contract employees.

Although wage costs have stabilized, benefit costs continue to increase. Health care costs have been increasing at double-digit levels every year for the last five years, and increases will continue for the foreseeable future. In addition, retirement costs pose a significant challenge for those organizations that offer defined benefit plans. Market returns have stagnated over the last five years, so many employers have had to fund shortfalls with cash contributions. And low interest rates, combined with low investment returns, have made it more difficult for companies to manage their pension costs.

Companies are demanding more measurement. HR-related costs, from salaries and benefits to technology to the day-to-day costs of running the HR function itself, are significant. Management everywhere wants to understand these costs and their return. How do benefits and salaries help attract and retain employees? What returns can the company expect for its training and development programs? In particular, management wants to know the return on investment of large HR capital projects such as administration outsourcing and technology expenditures. HR must also be able to provide managers with relevant measures that help them identify change in the organization, including factors such as patterns in attrition, performance management, career development, and employee satisfaction levels. By understanding these engagement levers, HR and leadership can develop ways to influence them.

Technology is now a given in HR. For many years, technology has been part of the HR landscape. But now, the range of technology-based solutions has created a more complex set of options for HR. The potential for streamlining tactical administrative services—including benefit enrollment and management, payroll, performance management, and record keeping—has increased exponentially. But these advances in technology also mean that employees in HR have to raise their game: greater and greater expertise in data management, analysis, database administration, and HRIS management is now expected of HR professionals in our organization.

Firm-specific realities must be taken into account. Towers Perrin also faced some internal factors that heavily influenced us as we rethought the HR function in 2001. First, at the end of 2000, as part of a planned succession, a new CEO was elected and a new senior leadership team appointed. While these changes were planned for and anticipated, the transition did bring new expectations into the executive suite. Consequently, our leadership developed and introduced a new business strategy in late 2001. Not surprisingly, this strategy was built around our mission, vision, and values, and as such was heavily dependent on our people. The new business strategy also meant a new type of HR support, which for us meant making some significant administrative, program, and strategic changes from the ground up. In a nutshell, we realized that we had to shore up the foundation of our HR house while extensively renovating every room.

First Things: Putting the HR House in Order

When I took over as managing director of human resources in 2001, one of the first things we looked at was our HR transactions. We discovered that we had too many people across the firm involved in processing and administering these transactions, and we had many people within HR doing highly administrative work. We believed that the work was being done inefficiently and that our service to employees and other stakeholders could be improved. By outsourcing some work and investing in technology, we were able to reduce costs and improve the quality of the service (in part because there were fewer hands). At the same time, we were able to insource some more strategic functions, in effect shifting the focus of our HR staff to more value-added work such as talent management.

To put our house in order, we focused on three areas:
1. Process reengineering and leveraging systems
2. Outsourcing for greater access to expertise
3. Insourcing in key areas: recruiting, communications and employee relations

Process Reengineering and Leveraging Systems

From a technology standpoint, we knew we had to look hard at our HRIS infrastructure and complete a PeopleSoft upgrade before the end of 2001. But we also had to focus on our core HR administration processes. In 2000, we had 150 PeopleSoft administrators, but no one was responsible for training or process documentation, and there was no clear process accountability. The administrative work, while necessary, did nothing to create value for our clients or help our management execute the firm's strategy.

Our human resources administration consultants had done some very thorough process documentation for us in early 2000, and they had created a detailed agenda for change. So we started a series of biweekly process reviews, bringing together staff from all our administrative areas to focus on how to improve each HR process. In these sessions, we questioned each step in the process, and as a result, we were able to identify some quick actions and changes in work processes that could be implemented even before we made changes to our HRIS. But these were only temporary measures. A lot of our process work led us to the fundamental HRIS issue we were confronting: that we would have to re-implement our PeopleSoft system.

We had been one of the earliest users of PeopleSoft, and over time we had made adjustments to the system coding to accommodate our needs. This had increased maintenance costs since we needed to staff ourselves with highly specialized expertise in running our own proprietary system. It also increased the complexity and cost of upgrades and migrations to newer versions of PeopleSoft.

We embarked on an aggressive, eight-month program to install a completely new PeopleSoft system. We knew that a successful transition would be one that no employee noticed. Our project was one of the most successful large-scale projects in the firm's history, due to strong management governance, excellent project management, and clear staff accountability across HR and other key units.

But that was only the beginning. We had to design an ongoing HR service delivery function that would ensure that processes were managed and updated. So in 2002 we piloted and in 2003 fully implemented a new HR service delivery network in which we consolidated full accountability for HR transaction processing and administration. We now have much greater consistency and standardization in core HR administration processing around the world. There are fewer ad hoc solutions being used in offices and countries; instead, we see wider acceptance of best practices within our far-flung organization. We are now confident that we can quickly disseminate the best possible processes in any area of HR transaction throughout our organization.

Outsourcing

We have also taken advantage of the outsourcing trend. HR outsourcing is pursued for many reasons, including cost and efficiency. However, the ROI is generally based on a high transaction volume. As a mid-sized global firm, we didn't have those high transaction levels, so our purpose in outsourcing was to gain access to process knowledge and expertise. For example, we used to administer domestic relocation and short-term disability in the United States ourselves, but we clearly could not provide the same kind of resources and technical knowledge that a specialist firm could. And since Towers Perrin is one of the leading providers of benefits administration ourselves, we were able to draw on our proprietary expertise in this area by outsourcing to our own benefits administration experts. While there were cost savings in making these transitions, the true goal was to increase service levels and gain access to best-practice capabilities.

Insourcing

The same goal—access to expertise at a reasonable cost—led us to insource our recruiting more extensively. In 2000, as much as 70 percent of our hiring was done through agencies. Today, that figure is about 30 percent. We made the change because we believed that we have a greater ability to work with our internal hiring managers and identify and acquire the talent we need. Although our decision to insource our recruiting has been helped by the vast reach of the Web, we believe that in our business, recruiting is not a transactional capability but a strategic one. It requires in-depth knowledge of the qualities, qualifications, and attributes that make a successful Towers Perrin employee, and that knowledge comes from working closely with our various businesses and business leaders.

Still, we hold our recruiting function to very tight metrics. We measure ROI annually by calculating the extent to which the recruiting infrastructure pays for itself in terms of both cash cost (avoiding retained search fees) and opportunity cost (more efficient use of our business managers' time).

As a rule of thumb, outsourcing is the best approach for transactional chores (e.g., benefits administration and record keeping) and for work that requires outside expertise or is too expensive or too infrequently used to keep in house (e.g., domestic and international relocation). We concluded that, in our case, strategic work and work that requires an in-depth and continually updated knowledge of the business (e.g., recruiting and employee relations) was probably best staffed from within the organization.

In parallel, we had to focus our attention on our rewards programs—including salary, benefits, training and development, and the work environment—and the "softer" factors that most directly influence employee engagement, such as organizational communications, recognition programs, performance management, and career management.

Moving to a Total Rewards Philosophy

During the same time period, we stepped back to assess the extent to which our rewards programs supported the firm's mission, vision, and values. We quickly concluded that we needed to restructure and upgrade our global pay and benefits structures to reflect the realities of the local employment markets within the context of a global rewards philosophy. Our goal was to ensure that all our rewards components supported a high-performance culture.

We developed a point of view on the portfolio of rewards we offered as a firm, including pay, variable pay, health and welfare benefits, and retirement benefits. In taking stock, we recognized two things: employee expectations regarding variable pay (primarily annual bonuses) had become detached from performance, and we were providing benefits that were above competitive market levels.

We took several steps to renew employee focus on the link between high performance and high rewards. On the pay side, rather than a one-size-fits-all global pay structure, we developed salary structures reflective of local market practices, especially regarding the mix of base salary and variable pay. We also made adjustments to our benefits programs to bring them more in line with competitive market practice. Our new programs give us the resources and flexibility to deliver higher rewards for our top performers. While the transition to a Total Rewards philosophy with a strong link to performance has not been easy, employee communication and sustained management dedication to our performance management approach have played a major role in helping employees understand that bonuses are not a given but are truly based on measurable performance. To be certain that our approach functions as intended, we continually benchmark and assess both the overall rewards program and its major elements.

Performance Management, Career Management

The success of our Total Rewards approach depended on efficient, measurable performance management and career management processes that were aligned with our rewards and clearly understood by our employees. In early 2001, we introduced a comprehensive career framework that provided detailed descriptions of responsibilities and competencies for every career level. This career framework links directly to our internal Towers Perrin Institute (learning and development) curriculum and to our Web-based career assessment tools, which employees and their managers use to monitor progress. We continually update the frameworks to reflect changes in our talent needs and our training programs.

We also support a full-circle feedback process for all employees, including our board of directors and senior leaders. This 360° process provides meaningful developmental data for our employees and leaders and is a critical tool in fostering a high-performance culture.

Recognition

Over the past several years, we have designed, revised, and implemented several new recognition programs:

Chairman's Award. This award is presented annually to employees who have been nominated by their peers as exemplifying our firm's mission, vision, and values. The firm's chairman and CEO, Mark Mactas, takes a personal interest in this annual nomination and award process. A special panel reviews all the peer nominations and makes recommendations to him. The award is presented personally by the CEO, and individual celebrations are held locally.

Executive Council Special Recognition bonuses. Each year the firm's senior leadership nominates candidates who have contributed to a cross-business or firmwide effort or who have made a significant contribution to the firm. Recipients receive monetary compensation and recognition on our intranet.

STARS awards. These monetary awards are specifically for non-bonus-eligible employees who have performed outstanding work. This recognition takes place any time during the year. These awards can be made by peers, by managers, or by employees themselves.

Driving Engagement through HR Best Practices

We have also helped foster employee engagement by establishing a more disciplined approach to many of our HR practices. Examples include the following:

Better recruiting and selection process. We have a very structured approach to sourcing and selection, which we developed about ten years ago and which we have been refining ever since. Our approach to sourcing is multi-faceted, with both long and short term perspectives in mind. For example, in the long term we know it is in our best interests, and that of our profession, to ensure that there is a solid pool of talent, from diverse backgrounds interested in entering our profession. We have a number of partnerships with professional societies, colleges and affinity groups where we do everything from provide coaching and mentoring to aspiring actuarial students; sponsor math contests; advise students on interviewing and resume preparation. With regard to short-term annual hiring needs, our employees are a key differentiating element of our success. Through networking and referrals, they provide the single largest source of non-campus hires. With their insights into who succeeds at our firm based on their daily experience, they assume a key role in identifying and screening the potential talent with whom they come into contact. Of course, we manage active university and mid-career level sourcing programs and, like many firms, we are aggressive users of the internet in sourcing and processing new hires. At the specific individual selection level, we use a combination of behaviorally based selection and screening approaches. We train all of our selection interviewers in these approaches, and offer 'refresher' courses on an ongoing basis. All of these elements are organized in a nine-step recruiting process that emphasizes professionalism, speed, and responsiveness in the way we treat candidates and provides them with a wealth of information about the firm. Several candidates have specifically cited our process as a reason for choosing Towers Perrin over our competitors.

Improved people manager training. Employees rely on their managers as a first line of information and depend on them for help ranging from performance and career management to answering questions about firm policies. Managers are also vital role models for our values of

- integrity,
- respect,
- and professionalism.

We have an active "Respect at Work" program in every office that helps raise the awareness of both managers and employees about the importance of different perspectives in the workplace and discusses how to maintain a positive, constructive environment for all our employees. We also offer an orientation program for managers that focuses on their roles, responsibilities, and best practices and has an increased focus on helping employees in overall career development.

Measuring Our Progress

The significant cost of HR and people-related programs has been on the radar of most management teams for some time now. At Towers Perrin, we have established detailed success measures for our recruiting, training and development, and HR service delivery operations. We have developed balanced scorecards to measure cost, productivity, and quality measures on a quarterly and annual basis, and we have linked these results, where appropriate, to the individual goals of HR staff members.

We also started a program to regularly measure employee engagement and obtain feedback on such programs as communication and performance management. Results of these Web-based surveys are reported to management and back to employees. Most important, we are able to compare our results to professional services industry norms and identify areas in which we are leading, and those which need improvement. Follow-up for these activities is a balance between firmwide and locally led actions.

Looking to the Future

We will continue to grapple with the conflicting pressures to control costs on the one hand and, on the other, to find ways to hire, develop, and reward the best from a shrinking talent pool. We continue to be more creative in how we access talent—through independent contracting, alliances, and other less traditional approaches. Of course, this raises the overall complexity of the task for HR and the management we support.

Cost pressures will require HR to continue to strive for best-practice standardization in a number of areas, especially benefits and pay programs. Doing so requires constant assessment of the trade-offs between efficiency and effectiveness. We, like many other companies, have made a strong commitment to Web-based employee and manager self-service. There are limits to this approach, however, particularly in a professional services environment, where time is so closely linked to revenues.

Today and in the near future, the keys for continued success in the HR arena include the following:

- Maintaining as smooth, cost-effective, and accurate an administrative function as possible
- Watching demographics closely and remaining flexible enough to develop staffing and hiring alternatives in multiple global markets
- Knowing the business well enough that HR is sought out as a valued participant on matters of *business* importance to the firm
- Measuring the success of HR functions—and the business implications—against a set of quantitative metrics
- Above all, serving as the firm's workplace conscience, no matter how uncomfortable or unpopular that makes you.

And, finally, a word about the people of HR. The significant changes within the HR function have created both stress and opportunity for HR staff. Days, typically, do not follow the predicted—sometimes a bit of the theater of the absurd, sometimes a bit of the emergency room—often rushed, never dull. The profile of the successful HR leadership team will require a balance of technical skill and business acumen, problem-solving and service orientation, and flexible design and disciplined process execution. And as personal attributes, add in deep reservoirs of energy and an infectious sense of humor. This will help ensure that HR is a role model for the best practices it espouses: a well-trained, well-managed, well-staffed, and highly engaged team.

Anne Donovan Bodnar is Managing Director of Human Resources at Towers Perrin and has been with the Firm since 1985.

Prior to her work in corporate, she was a consultant for eight years in Towers Perrin's HR Services business, leading competitive positioning assignments for global multinationals in a wide arrange of industries. She was honored by the Firm with her election to the YWCA's Academy of Women Achievers in 1999.

Earlier in her career, she worked in operational and strategic planning roles at large financial services firms.

Mrs. Bodnar graduated from Smith College, cum laude, Phi Beta Kappa, in 1978, with B.A. degree in Government and French. She also has an M.B.A. from Harvard Business School (1985).

She lives in New York City with her husband, Jim, an architect, and her two daughters, Katharine, 14 and Mary Anne, 10.

I would like to dedicate this chapter to the employees of Towers Perrin, whose outstanding commitment to client service and professional excellence continues to inspire us in Human Resources to set and strive for high levels of achievement. In particular I salute the firm's hard working, dedicated HR staff.

Acknowledgment: *In writing this chapter, I would like to acknowledge the contributions of my colleagues Nancy Connors and J. David Dean.*

C-Level Quarterly Journal
What Every Executive Needs to Know

The Quarterly Journal Written by C-Level (CEO, CFO, CTO, CMO, Partner) Executives from the World's Top Companies

The objective of C-Level is to enable you to cover all your knowledge bases and be kept abreast of critical business information and strategies by the world's top executives. Each quarterly issue features articles on the core areas of which every executive must be aware, in order to stay one step ahead - including management, technology, marketing, finance, operations, ethics, law, hr and more. Over the course of the year, C-Level features the thinking of executives from over half the Global 500 and other leading companies of all types and sizes. While other business publications focus on the past, or current events, C-Level helps executives stay one step ahead of major business trends that are occurring 6 to 12 months from now.

Sample C-Level Executive Contributors/Subscribers Include:

Advanced Fibre Communications, Akin Gump Strauss Hauer & Feld, American Express, American Standard Companies, AmeriVest Properties, A.T. Kearney, AT&T Wireless, Bank of America, Barclays, BDO Seidman, BearingPoint (Formerly KPMG Consulting), BEA Systems, Bessemer Ventures, Best Buy, BMC Software, Boeing, Booz-Allen Hamilton, Boston Capital Ventures, Burson-Marsteller, Corning, Countrywide, Cravath, Swaine & Moore, Credit Suisse First Boston, Deutsche Bank, Dewey Ballantine, Duke Energy, Ernst & Young, FedEx, Fleishman-Hilliard, Ford Motor Co., General Electric, Hogan & Hartson, IBM, Interpublic Group, Jones, Day, Reavis & Pogue Ketchum, KPMG, LandAmerica, Leo Burnett, Mack-Cali Realty Corporation, Merrill Lynch, Micron Technology, Novell, Office Depot, Ogilvy & Mather, On Semiconductor, Oxford Health, PeopleSoft, Perot Systems, Prudential, Ropes & Gray, Saatchi & Saatchi, Salomon Smith Barney, Staples, TA Associates, Tellabs, The Coca-Cola Company, Unilever, Verizon, VoiceStream Wireless, Webster Financial Corporation, Weil, Gotshal & Manges, Yahoo!, Young & Rubicam

Subscribe & Become a Member of C-Level
Only $219.95/Year for 4 Quarterly Issues

Call 1-866-Aspatore or Visit www.Aspatore.com to Order

Other Best Sellers

Visit Your Local Bookseller Today or www.Aspatore.com
for a Complete Title List

- Ninety-Six and Too Busy to Die - Life Beyond the Age of Dying - $24.95

- Technology Blueprints - Strategies for Optimizing and Aligning Technology Strategy and Business - $69.95

- The CEO's Guide to Information Availability - Why Keeping People and Information Connected is Every Leader's New Priority - $27.95

- Being There Without Going There - Managing Teams Across Time Zones, Locations and Corporate Boundaries - $24.95

- Profitable Customer Relationships - CEOs from Leading Software Companies on using Technology to Maxmize Acquisition, Retention and Loyalty - $27.95

- The Entrepreneurial Problem Solver - Leading CEOs on How to Think Like an Entrepreneur and Solve Any Problem for Your Team/Company - $27.95

- The Philanthropic Executive - Establishing a Charitable Plan for Individuals and Businesses - $27.95

- The Golf Course Locator for Business Professionals - Organized by Closest to Largest 500 Companies, Cities and Airports - $12.95

- Living Longer Working Stronger - 7 Steps to Capitalizing on Better Health - $14.95

- Business Travel Bible - Must Have Phone Numbers, Business Resources, Maps and Emergency Info- $19.95

- ExecRecs - Executive Recommendations for the Best Business Products and Services Professionals Use to Excel - $14.95

Call 1-866-Aspatore or Visit www.Aspatore.com to Order